Wayne Buchanan

He trained as an actor at Oval House Youth Theatre. His theatre credits include: *Bitter and Twisted*, *Zumbi*, and *Temporary Rupture* (Black Theatre Co-op), *Nine Night* (Umoja), *Foxtrot in the Sand* (African People's Theatre) and *Two* (Oval House).

His writing credits are: *Vengeance* staged in 1998, nominated for an EMMA Award and voted best play of 1998 by The New Nation newspaper. His second play *Under Their Influence* was first staged in May 2000 at Oval House Theatre and received *Time Out Critics' Choice*.

He is one of the founders of *Kushite Theatre Company*.

aurora metro press

Founded in 1989 to publish and promote new writing, the press has specialised in new drama and fiction, winning recognition and awards from the industry.

new drama

Black and Asian Plays Anthology, introduced by Afia Nkrumah ISBN 0-9536757-4-2 £9.95

Six plays by Black and Asian women. ed. Kadija George ISBN 0-9515877-2-2 £7.50

Best of the Fest. new plays celebrating 10 years of London New Play Festival ed. Phil Setren ISBN 0-9515877-8-1 £12.99

Young Blood, five plays for young performers. ed. Sally Goldsworthy ISBN 0-9515877-6-5 £9.95

Plays for Young People, Charles Way ISBN 0-9536757- 1-8 £9.95

Seven plays by women, female voices, fighting lives. ed. Cheryl Robson ISBN 0-9515877-1-4 £5.95

Three Plays, Jonathan Moore ISBN 0-9536757-2-6 £9.95

Kushite Theatre Company present

Under Their Influence

by Wayne Buchanan

AURORA METRO PRESS

Trade distribution:

UK - Central Books Tel: 020 8986 4854

USA – T.C.G., N.Y. Tel: 212 697 5230

Canada – Playwrights Union of Canada Tel: 416 703 0201

ISBN 0-9536757-5-0 Printed by Antony Rowe, Chippenham

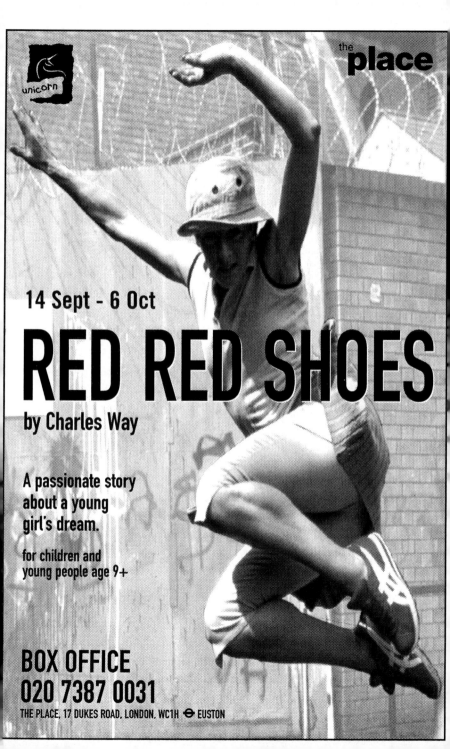

<u>Under Their Influence on tour</u>

3-15 SEP   **Tricycle Theatre**, London, 8pm
BO 020 7328 1000
Tickets: from £8.50

26-28 SEP   **The Green Room**, Manchester 8pm
BO 0161 615 0500
Tickets: £7.00/£4.00 conc.

29 SEP   **Theatre in the Mill**, Bradford, 7.30pm
BO 01274 233 200
Tickets: £8.50/£4.00 conc.

3 OCT   **South Street Arts Ctre**, Reading 8pm
BO 0118 960 6060
Tickets: £6.00

6 OCT   **Nottingham Playhouse**, 8pm
BO 0115 941 9419
Tickets: £8.00/ £5.00

Introducing Kushite Theatre Company

Established in 1998 with its first production, *Vengeance* at
the Oval House Theatre, a tragic story of child abuse and
how it shapes its adult survivors, it was subsequently
nominated for an EMMA award and selected as Best Play
of 1998 by the New Nation newspaper. *Under Their
Influence* was first produced in May 2000, featured on
Newsnight, published by Aurora Metro Press in *Black and
Asian Plays Anthology* and was *Time Out Critics' Choice.*
Gods and Bad Guys by Tunde Euba in October 2000 was a
co-production with Oval House, a slapstick comedy about
an international failed drug dealer from Lagos.

Currently in development: *Search for the Moor* by Wayne
Buchanan, *Made in Heaven* by Sesun Ogunledun and *Front
Room* by Jenny Davies.

Kushite Theatre Company takes its name from an
ancient African dynasty that presided over an empire that
spanned the three continents of Africa, South Asia and
Western Europe for 3,000 years from approximately
10,000 BC. The Kushites were the true pioneers of the
theatre, predecessors of the Greeks with a renowned
reputation for constantly striving for excellence. They
implemented a system of egalitarianism, which
acknowledged difference, engaged in cultural exchange and
embraced the growth of the diversity that constituted their
empire. The company takes this name because it
endeavours to embrace these inspiring principles of
excellence, equality, and pioneering spirit in the art that it
creates.

Biographies

Antonia Beamish trained at American Academy of Dramatic Arts. Theatre credits include: *On Tidy Endings,* Judi Dench Theatre, *Educating Rita,* international tour, *Principia,* New York Theatre Workshop, *Look back in Anger,* Classic Stage Company NY, *The Corner Bar Is My Lover,* Here NY Archaos Circus, international tour. Film credits: *Dead Creatures,* dir. Andrew Parkinson *Love,* dir. Dominique Margot, *Mexico Mocumentry,* Calmexcine, LA. *15 Months in May* dir. Anya Muman

Wayne Buchanan trained as an actor at Oval House Youth Theatre. His theatre credits include: *Bitter and Twisted,* *Zumbi,* and *Temporary Rupture* (Black Theatre Co-op), *Nine Night* (Umoja), *Fox-trot in the Sand* (African People's Theatre) and *Two* (Oval House). His writing credits are: *Vengeance,* staged in 1998 nominated for an EMMA award and voted best play of 1998 by The New Nation newspaper.

Karena Johnson has an MA in theatre direction, University of London. Theatre credits include: *Two* by Jim Cartwright, *Ever Been* devised by JAWA, *May* by Jackie Cobham, *Vengeance* and *Under Their Influence* by Wayne Buchanan, *Gods and Bad Guys* by Tunde Euba, *Under The Sky* by Grant Buchanan Marshall (reading). Other credits: Associate Producer at the *NOW ninety8* and Nottingham Playhouse, Associate Director at Oval House Theatre and Theatre Royal, Stratford East and is currently Head of Theatre Programming at Oval House Theatre and Artistic Director of *Kushite Theatre Company.*

Michael Rochester trained at the Academy of Performing Arts. Theatre Credits include: *Anthony and Cleopatra,* dir. Vanessa Redgrave, *Macbeth,* dir. Mark Hillier, *Song of an Honouree Soul Man,* dir. Roger Watkin, *Firebird,* Unicorn Theatre, *Magic Storybook.* TV and Film credits: *Wycliffe,* HTV, *Open for business* and *Island whisper* BBC, *Sweet Skin Life,*

Twenty Pieces of Glass, Mark Grave productions, *I want you,* dir. Michael Winterbottom: *Not without the Nome (Cannes short film festival nomination.)*

Natalie Tinn trained at Mountview Theatre School. Theatre credits include: Young New Writer's, Soho Theatre, *Hijra,* Bush Theatre, *Inkle and Yarico,* Sadlers Wells international tour to US, Barbados, *Made in England,* BAC and Etcetra, *Peter Pan,* Royal National Theatre, *Smokey Joe's Café,* Prince of Wales, *Fame,* The Cambridge, *Carol* Tristan Bates Theatre, *Gratuitous Sex & Violence,* Millfield, *Jack and the Beanstalk* and *Cinderella,* Theatre Royal, Stratford East. TV & film credits: *Oscar Charlie,* BBC, *What Rats Won't Do,* Working Title, *Douglas* BBC, *Welcome to London* EFS TV

Charlie Folorunsho Since leaving Rose Bruford in 1991 Charlie has worked extensively in theatre. The first play he did was for TEMBA THEATRE Company 'A Killing Passion', then 'A False Servant' at The Gate Theatre, 'Peter Pan' The Crucible, 'Romeo and Juliette' 'Arabian Night's' 'Gil Gamesh' 'Alladin' 'The Giraffe and 'The Pelly and Me' all for The London Bubble, 'The Lower Depths' Cardboard Citz, 'Faust' English Shakespeare Co, 'The Mosquito Coast' for David Glass at The Young Vic, 'Tales Form Home' for The Besht Tellers at The Tricycle, 'Alls Well That Ends Well' Oxford Stage Co, 'The Island' Theatre Clywd, 'Pinnocchio' at The Salisbury Theatre, 'Brave New World' and 'Moby Dick' for The American Drama Group in Europe, 'Gilgamesh' The Opera Factory and most recently 'Passports to the Promised Land' for Nitro Theatre Co. Charlie has also sung in funk bands and has much workshop experience

Delon Watson trained at Guildhall School of Music & Drama. TV credits include: *London's Burning,* BBC, *Murder in Mind,* BBC, *Plato's Breaking Point.* Theatre credits include: *Teachers,* and *Midsummer Nights Dream,* Nuffield Theatre, *Colour of Justice,* Tricycle Theatre national tour. Delon appeared in the original cast of *Under Their Influence,* Kushite Theatre Company.

Under Their Influence

The play was first written in 1996. I stopped writing it to produce my first play *Vengeance* with the help of director Karena Johnson. *Under Their Influence* has been through many rewrites as I worked with the dramaturg at Oval House, Paul Everitt. The process has been long and at times, painful. Like the characters in the play, I've often felt frustrated but thanks to the ancestors and to those who doubted my ability, I was determined to persevere. My hard work has paid off, as the play opened at Oval House Theatre for a four week run and was Critic's Choice in *Time Out* Magazine. It has been generally well-received by the Press and featured on the BBC's *Newsnight* programme and many radio stations. This is our second production and tour to regional venues.

The Play

Under Their Influence is a thriller set in contemporary London. The action takes place in a mental institution where the patient is having what he hopes is his final assessment. Randoulf takes his psychiatrist on a journey she does not anticipate, hoping that she will see him as an individual rather than a bunch of clinical symptoms to be controlled. As Doctor Kumar is taken on this trip, we see and feel the internal workings of Randoulf, his political views, his passions, his weaknesses, his pain and vulnerability. We meet some of his friends, lovers and most important of all, his alter ego.

Wayne Buchanan

Under Their Influence

by Wayne Buchanan

First performed at the Oval House Theatre, Kennington, in May 2000. This new production opened at the Tricycle Theatre, Kilburn in September 2001 with the following cast, before touring nationally.

Director	Karena Johnson
Designer	Libby Watson
Lighting Designer	Tina MacHugh
Co. Stage Manager	Lizzie Chapman
Asst. Stage Manager	Gianni Bettucci
Lighting Operator	Simon Garcia
Video	Saria Ofogba
Producer	Sarah Moore
Press Officer	Esther Armah

CHARACTERS	CAST
Randoulf	Wayne Buchanan
Randoulf 2	Charlie Folorunsho
Doctor Kumar	Natalie Tinn
Nicole	Antonia Beamish
Josephine	Delon Watson
Julian	Michael Rochester
Video:	
Nurse	Jasper Hone
Mother	Angela Wynter
Guard 1	David Rivette
Guard 2	Patrick Kilian
Young Randoulf	Zuri Jarrett
Police Officer 1	Des Hegarty
Police Officer 2	Rupert Blake
Guards	Marlon Bulger, Steve Gibbs, Matt Jamie

ACT ONE
SCENE 1

A cell in a mental institution. The cell is completely white except for the sink, toilet, mirror and wash basin, which are stainless-steel. A table, chair and bed are bolted to the floor. A four inch pipe runs round the wall as a heating system and a form of communication. There is a window on the back wall with bars but not prison-like. Books, radio, and toiletries can be seen immaculately placed on top of a chest of draws.

Enter female Doctor and male Nurse.

RANDOULF	Can I help you?
DOCTOR	I believe you're expecting us.
RANDOULF	That's news to me.
DOCTOR	Doctor Goldberg has been taken ill...
RANDOULF	I can wait until he returns.
DOCTOR	I'm afraid he will not be back for a while.
RANDOULF	I don't mind waiting three or four days.
DOCTOR	Doctor Goldberg has other engagements.
RANDOULF	I said I'll wait.

(Nurse moves behind him)

DOCTOR	We are sorry for this sudden change of pattern.
RANDOULF	Why was I not informed of the situation promptly?

(Doctor moves next to panic button. Nurse moves a syringe from his top pocket to his thigh pocket)

DOCTOR   We have informed you of the situation at the earliest possible notice. *(indicates for Nurse to* *accompany her)* Let's start again. Good morning, Randoulf. My name is Doctor Kumar.

RANDOULF   Good morning...

DOCTOR   And this is Nurse Beverbrook.

RANDOULF   Good morning, Nurse Beverbrook.

DOCTOR   Been sleeping well?

RANDOULF   Better than last week... and yourself, have you been sleeping well?

DOCTOR   Always do Randoulf, always do.
(Male Nurse sits behind Doctor)

RANDOULF   You have been briefed well.

DOCTOR   We are fully staffed.

RANDOULF   I have noticed.

DOCTOR   You know why I am here?

RANDOULF   No. *(He hits himself on his forehead with the palm of his hand)* I mean yes, but this is a mental institution and wires do get crossed sometimes, do they not?

DOCTOR   Yes.

RANDOULF   I believe you being here has something to do with my faculties... Right?

DOCTOR   You... something like that. Twice a year we review your C.P.A. to see how you're developing.

RANDOULF   I'm approximately the same size I was when I arrived here, give or take a few pounds. *(He models for her)* Wouldn't you say?

DOCTOR   We're talking about your state of mind not your body.

RANDOULF   How many times must I tell you people, there is nothing wrong with my mind.

DOCTOR   These sessions will help me assess if you are no longer a risk to yourself or the public. We may release you into the community.

RANDOULF   Wow-wee.

DOCTOR   Your Prime Minister brought that
benefit to you.

RANDOULF   I always knew Tony was too clever for
his own good.

DOCTOR   It wasn't his deed – it was the Iron
Lady. *(Randoulf tenses up)* It's called, 'Care in the
Community'. Relax. She had a thing about integration.

RANDOULF   How many drugs or pharmaceutical
products are going to be tested on me for that privilege?

DOCTOR   This will be an honest assessment. No
medication will be needed. *(He looks at her oddly)* We
want you in a natural state, so to speak.

RANDOULF   I was looking forward to some pink,
blue, purple and yellow sweets.

DOCTOR   You have a great sense of humour…

RANDOULF   Who wouldn't in a place like this?

DOCTOR   Admittedly one is needed.

RANDOULF   I thought I saw and heard everything
while I was out there but since I've been a resident here,
I've come to the conclusion that we in here are the wise
and they out there, are the misguided.

DOCTOR   What do you mean?

RANDOULF   Everyone believes they are smart or
knowledgeable but they only know what they know and
not about what they don't know.

DOCTOR *(thinks)* You're quite a character.
(She flips open his file)

RANDOULF   I bet you're an interesting character.

DOCTOR   You were imprisoned in nineteen ninety
six for murder. Six months later you were moved here
and stabilised with drugs and according to Dr Goldberg
… psychotherapy has been beneficial.

RANDOULF   You tell a beautiful tale but you've been
misled on one very important matter. *(She walks over to*

his bed and runs her hand over the bedhead looking for dust)

DOCTOR   If I stand to be corrected, correct me.

RANDOULF   A crime of passion – if you don't mind. *(He checks the bed also)*

DOCTOR   To be *(reading)*... released when no longer a threat to the public.

RANDOULF   I'm no harm to anyone but myself.

DOCTOR   I don't know that Randoulf. I don't know that.

RANDOULF   Really? *(She stands by the chair)*

DOCTOR   Mind if I sit down?

RANDOULF   Be my guest. *(He bows)*

DOCTOR   Thank you.

RANDOULF   One of us has to treat the other like a human being. *(She takes out a tape-recorder)*

DOCTOR   Everything you and I say will be recorded. It's for accuracy.

RANDOULF   Everybody wants tape recordings and video films for evidence. *(He turns to face her)* Many years ago, that would have benefited thousands of sisters and brothers, who now have criminal records because of racist people disguising themselves as law enforcers...

DOCTOR   When you're ready.

RANDOULF   You don't care do you?

DOCTOR   I have no jurisdiction to comment on things I have no evidence to prove.

RANDOULF   So you have to be a member of the Bar to comment on such matters... I never saw one Israeli slaughtered but I know something horrific happened.

DOCTOR   Historical facts are facts. *(A beat)*

RANDOULF   I haven't seen one black woman or man being whipped, lynched or burnt for fun... women's bellies being sliced open for the unborn child to feed the appetites of sharks... but I know it hurts the whole world because nobody likes talking about it, for they are all guilty...

DOCTOR   Are you alright, Randoulf?

RANDOULF   Sure I am. Can't you see? By the way I have no intellectual jurisdiction on the matter but my skin colour informs me of people's behaviour.

DOCTOR   When you're ready.
(He sits on the frame of the bed)

RANDOULF   Where would you like me to begin?

DOCTOR   How about the beginning?

RANDOULF   There are many beginnings. Which one?

DOCTOR   How about the one that put you here?
(She writes)

RANDOULF   Are you married?

DOCTOR   I'm not the one being assessed.

RANDOULF   Of all the doctors in the world they send me a woman. *(He laughs wickedly)* This must be deliberate.

DOCTOR *(writes)* Would you care to elaborate?

RANDOULF   I'm sitting in your body, right, and I'm looking at me.

DOCTOR   What do you see?

RANDOULF   A pitiful sight of a man. *(He leans towards her)* It's like you have me all tied up.

DOCTOR   That type of thing isn't for me.

RANDOULF   You're no different from any other human being.

DOCTOR   Maybe so...

RANDOULF   You have the same desires as men... the only difference between us is that you give birth ... how I wish I had that ability. *(She writes frantically and he walks to her left. He turns to Nurse)* Let me tell you something about women which I know you can identify with. *(Nurse drops pen and picks it up. Cigarette packet drops from his top pocket to the floor)* I hope you had no intention of polluting my space.

DOCTOR   I...

RANDOULF   I hate smokers. They're so selfish. Come with me for a minute. *(He closes his eyes then opens them)* Close your eyes then. He's cautious... tell him it will be fine. *(She nods to Nurse)* ... good, I'm going to the toilet...

DOCTOR   Why are you taking him to the toilet?

RANDOULF   To shit of course and he's coming with me to sample the perfume.

DOCTOR   Is that how unpleasant smoking is to you?

RANDOULF   Worse! When you leave the toilet you don't smell of shit! *(Nurse opens his eyes)*

DOCTOR   Shall we continue?

RANDOULF   Yes. Let's not lose our objective. *(He walks around)* Now where was I?

DOCTOR *(prompts him)* Let me tell you something... *(She reads)* ... about women which you can identify with.

RANDOULF   You can give a woman everything she wants but she'll never be happy until she captures your soul. *(She studies him)* I know that goes for men too, but in a different way.

DOCTOR   Elaborate.

RANDOULF   Men want women to need them financially, to do things around the house, and show off their testosterone.

DOCTOR   You think women want men's physical strength?

RANDOULF   Yes.

DOCTOR   Interesting.

RANDOULF   You travel with me this time... Just relax, like you do at home. *(She stretches her legs in front of her)* Every woman wants a healthy man to reproduce with, but if another man makes advances and he defends her honour, then she allows her defender to take her to bed.

DOCTOR   Why?

RANDOULF   Possession of her mind, soul and body but in reverse.

DOCTOR   So from your point of view – women want your soul. *(Long beat)*

RANDOULF   There is something spiritual about women because they give birth to life. That makes them special. *(She writes)* You can give her a car, a boat, a house but all these are nothing compared to your soul. She will drive the car, decorate the house while admiring the boat but these things can't see her and her seductive shape. *(He shifts his attention to the Nurse)* I bet you buy your wife things to confuse her? *(He looks at the Doctor then back to the Nurse who just sits there)* Speak, she won't say anything. See what I mean?… a simple question and he's frightened to offend. *(He walks away)* To be in command of someone is a powerful thing. Altering her appearance is something she is very skilled at. If she puts on lipstick it affects you – you the man. Just looking into your eyes she can read you like a book. *(He stops before the Doctor)* That is the only time in her life that she'll ever feel secure with a man... when she knows she has his soul. After all – we came from woman and not the other way around, as some would have us believe. *(He turns his attention to the Nurse)* I see you're just here to listen.

DOCTOR   I detect a little resentment. *(A beat)* Do you like women?

RANDOULF And they give *you* the job to compile the final report? *(Silence)* The ones I loved all had ready-made families... *(He thinks)* ... and it took a woman to bring that to my attention... *(a change of tone)* ... as well.

DOCTOR Was that a problem?

RANDOULF No, don't get me wrong. I'm not complaining. I only mention this because most men will have relationships with women who have children but won't settle down with them.

DOCTOR What reason would you put that down to?

RANDOULF They're frightened of the footsteps of the other man.

DOCTOR And the reason for this lack of commitment?

RANDOULF There is something about a race of people who are born in conjunction with slavery.

DOCTOR I don't understand.

RANDOULF They seem to breed generations of bastards!

DOCTOR Are *you* illegitimate Randoulf? *(A beat)*

RANDOULF I don't know.

DOCTOR If you're illegitimate –

RANDOULF I said I don't know!... and I'm not saying she lied to me either!

DOCTOR I would never suggest anything of the kind.

RANDOULF Then what are you implying?

DOCTOR Your mother...

RANDOULF What about her?

DOCTOR Would you say she was a happy woman?

RANDOULF   Not as happy as she would have liked, considering she never had a man around to share the burden of raising me.

DOCTOR   They were hard times?

RANDOULF   She worked like a slave. *(She writes)*

DOCTOR   What was your mother's occupation?

RANDOULF   She was into domestics.

DOCTOR   She was a cleaner?

RANDOULF   At five in the morning she would be on the road, on her way to clean offices. Then she would start again at nine, cooking for students… She was always on her feet. When she came home she was on her feet again cooking our kind of food while talking to me. *(A beat)*

DOCTOR   The things she said?

RANDOULF   She expressed her dislike towards men who just fuck and leave. Those who won't stay and look after their children. "Invest in them and not *Tennants, Special Brew, Shergar* and *Red Rum*." These things she would often feed me, so I would do better when I had her grandchildren.

DOCTOR   How did you know she was right?

RANDOULF   My mother is always right. *(She writes)* First and foremost, I must treat their mother not like my father treated *her*. *(He withdraws into himself)* I must work, feed, and nurture my children as if they were myself.

He hears his Mother's voice and they speak together. Then we see the Mother and Young Randoulf.

MOTHER/RANDOULF   Worship them as they do their mother.

RANDOULF   Defend your woman at all times.

DOCTOR   Even if she's wrong?

RANDOULF   I will correct her when we get home, or in private.

MOTHER/RANDOULF   Don't keep any woman on the side. Promise me.

DOCTOR   Did you? (*She waits for his answer*)

YOUNG RANDOULF   Yes. (*Mother touches him*)

MOTHER   Look at your community and see how they live like slaves. (*She kneels*) I don't want that for you.

YOUNG RANDOULF   I will never live like a slave Mummy.

MOTHER   I know.

Mother and Young Randoulf disappear.

DOCTOR   Do you believe your people live like slaves?

RANDOULF *(ponders)* We not only live like slaves, we behave like them.

DOCTOR   How?

RANDOULF *(looks at the space where his Mother was)* She would tell me how they used to live on the plantation. Feeding us pork as a way of cutting us away from our God. *(stands)* The plantation was a place for studding out our men to yield an abundance of children. Our women were used as breeding chambers. Our responsibility was to care for and love their children, but if given the choice to lavish our own with the same love and affection, we leave them and their mothers to fend for themselves. Our women are no better. They walk around with everything on display... they are fed fashion like dolls... they wear anything that will debase us.

DOCTOR   Do you like women?

.F   I was indoctrinated to love and respect

               So why the scorn?

RANDOULF   I gave it all and all they did was take.

DOCTOR   Were they in need? *(He drops his head)*

RANDOULF   Yes. *(disgusted with himself)* I made promises to my mother and her situation.

DOCTOR   How about living for yourself Randoulf?

RANDOULF *(ignores the question)* I'd buy them quality – that would include the children... that I did because... *(He trails off.)*

DOCTOR   Of your mother's situation?

The Mother reappears.

RANDOULF   We all benefited. *(He turns his back on his mother)* You should have seen the look on the mothers' faces.

DOCTOR   What kind of look was that?

RANDOULF *(shame again)* Appreciation and thanks.

MOTHER *(walks towards him)* Don't scorn a woman because she has children for another man. *(She lifts up his head by his chin)* That hatred must be saved for the men who abandon their children.

DOCTOR   You don't sound like the plantation slave you say you are.

RANDOULF   You only know half of me.

DOCTOR   What do you mean?
(The Mother fades out. Randoulf bows his head in shame again) Where is your mother?

RANDOULF   Why do you want to know?

DOCTOR   I need to have a detailed picture of you for the records. *(He turns his back.)*

RANDOULF	She's in America. *(She looks at the file)*
DOCTOR	Where in America?
RANDOULF	Last I heard, she was in Detroit.
DOCTOR	Why are you lying?
RANDOULF	You already know where she is, so why provoke me?
DOCTOR	I'm not intending to provoke you...

RANDOULF *(faces her)* She's in the same environment as I.

DOCTOR	What environment is that Randoulf?
RANDOULF	We are both in the loony bin.
DOCTOR	Why is *she* there?
RANDOULF	She cared and loved too much.
DOCTOR	Your father?
RANDOULF	Yes! *(They lock eyes)* Satisfied?

DOCTOR Not that you're upset. I need to ask these questions and I would like you to trust me.

RANDOULF I don't feel like conversing anymore. *(He walks over to his bed)* I want to be by myself.

A bell rings. Randoulf 2, his alter ego, appears from under the bed. Both he and Randoulf look sharply at the door.

RANDOULF Who the fuck is that? *(He creeps to the door and looks though the spy hole)*

RANDOULF 2 Mi noh know but wid one gess mi cyaan tell yuh.

RANDOULF Why do people always come and see me when I don't invite them?

RANDOULF 2 *(leaps onto the bed)* Because yuh is a easy ketch.

RANDOULF   Well, they can stay outside for being so unreasonable. *(He walks back to bed)* Unsociable bastard.

RANDOULF 2   Yes, mek dem tan out deh.

RANDOULF   And a woman at that.

RANDOULF 2   Wise move.

RANDOULF   All they want to do is come here and tempt me.

RANDOULF 2   Now yuh tarking an tinking as mi. Aal dem waan fi doh is tempt wi. *(jumps off the bed and conjures up what he wants Randoulf to see.)*

RANDOULF   You know something, you're absolutely right. I must listen to you more often.

The Doctor stands and walks towards him, looking for who he's talking to.

RANDOULF 2   Mi cyaan juss imagine weh shi hav arn. *(He walks over to where the Doctor was sitting and sits)* A coat weh swing wid her wen shi wark, anda-neat tight fitting garments an wen shi peel dem aaf like, like one a dem reptile a shed skin.
(The Doctor is fascinated. The Doctor and Randoulf 2 cross paths) Lard a wen shi sidong an crass her foot. *(Randoulf sits and crosses his legs like Randoulf 2)* … knowing full well yarh look pan dem. A personally wouldn't waan her in ya eeda. Sit up. Sit up. *(He does)* Now shake dat image out ta yuh head. *(He does)* It gone?

RANDOULF   Yes.

RANDOULF 2   Stap tell lie, shake it again. It gone now?

RANDOULF   Yes.

RANDOULF 2   Siit deh an don't mek it reoccur again. Right?

RANDOULF   Right. (*Randoulf 2 freezes*)

DOCTOR   Randoulf... Randoulf... I didn't mean to upset you.

RANDOULF   I just like being by myself. (*He's back in the present*) That day she came... I did well that day. Yes I was proud of myself. *(sits on the floor, Randoulf 2 mimics him)* I congratulated myself with a large dash of white rum. It was then it started...

From off-stage we hear the sounds of screaming and running.

RANDOULF 2 *(unfreezes)* Black man a beat up im woman again. Im run fram di National Front, di Ku Klux Klan but kick shit out-ta somebaddy weh look like im an im madda.

We hear voices from off-stage. Then Julian and Josephine appear.

JULIAN   A fought you said you was gonna be back by nine?

JOSEPHINE   Not tonight Julian.

JULIAN   Whad ya mean not tonight?

JOSEPHINE   I'm tired, hungry, frustrated from a hard day's work.

JULIAN   You're frustrated? Where ya bin?

JOSEPHINE   Julian.

JULIAN   Where ya bin?

JOSEPHINE   Shopping.

JULIAN   Every fucking time you're late, shopping is your fucking excuse. You muss fink I'm a fucking idiot.

JOSEPHINE   I got caught in traffic.

JULIAN   Wiv who?

JOSEPHINE   Another hundred and ten passengers on
the bus.

JULIAN   Really?

JOSEPHINE   Honestly.

JULIAN   Come here. I said come here.

JOSEPHINE   Don't hurt me Julian.

JULIAN   I won't.

JOSEPHINE   You're gripping me too hard, Julian.

JULIAN   What?

JOSEPHINE   Not now… my body isn't ready for
you…

JULIAN   Don't talk shit!

JOSEPHINE   Julian!

JULIAN   You go to the gym, tone up your body,
firm up your thighs and expect no reaction from me?

JOSEPHINE   No! Julian, please. Julian no! (*She fights
him*) Julian please. No! No! No! Ahhhhhrrrr!
Ahhhhhrrrr! Jesus Christ, help me!

JULIAN   You can't .You can't have kids. What
kind of fucking woman are you anyway…? You should
feel ashamed.

Randoulf turns on his radio.

RANDOULF 2   Bess ting fi do, drown dem out bastard,
dats aal yuh cyaan caal im. Six foot taal an bill like a
shit house. Im a put im han pan people gal pickney.
Bring back slavery an lynch di bastard.

RANDOULF   Is that the way men talk to women?

RANDOULF 2   Yuh waan confirmation fram mi?

RANDOULF   What a thing to say to a woman.

RANDOULF 2   Dis man is a bad man. Shi muss…
(*There's laughter coming from off-stage. Randoulf turns the radio down*) A weh di rahtid a gwan dong deh? One minute im a drap lick pan her, di next, di two a dem a laugh lakka puss.

RANDOULF   I can't believe it.
(*He takes a glass and puts it on the floor, to listen*)

JULIAN   Gimme your soul.

JOSEPHINE   You're not worthy of it.

JULIAN   Gimme it.

JOSEPHINE   No.

JULIAN   One night you'll give it me.

JOSEPHINE   Ohhh, Julian. I won't.

RANDOULF 2   Im deh pan her again?

RANDOULF (*listens intently*) Shhhhh! (*The Doctor walks around Randoulf. Randoulf 2 puts his ear to the ground*) I should go down and give her some assistance.

RANDOULF 2   Keep out ta it yuh hear papa. (*standing*)

RANDOULF   Do you think we should be more neighbourly?

RANDOULF 2   Wi doing alright by wi self.

RANDOULF   Listen…

RANDOULF 2   If yuh goh dong deh, di two a dem would da tong pan yuh an beat yuh up.

RANDOULF   What she sees in him, I don't know.

RANDOULF 2   Shi like most woman – dem like man wid sweet tongue. A juss soh dem function. (*Randoulf moves to the window*) Is natural fi yuh waan fi help a woman een distress but me narh goh allow yuh fi open yuhself toh bad influences.

RANDOULF   There she goes to buy him the poisonous *Tennants*. (*He ducks out of sight*) Jesus she's seen me.

RANDOULF 2   Now shi a goh tell her man.

RANDOULF   Tell him what?

RANDOULF 2   Di laas ting yuh waan is a woman fi goh get yuh een na fight.

RANDOULF *(paces up and down)* Calm down, calm down. What can she say? *(He puts the glass away)*

RANDOULF 2   Noting.

RANDOULF   Exactly.

RANDOULF 2   If shi brok good.

RANDOULF   She's beautiful.

RANDOULF 2 *(studies Randoulf for a good while)* Weh yuh seh?

RANDOULF   She looks harmless. How can he hit someone so fragile?

RANDOULF 2   Look, here's a good book about stars like Sirius-B…

RANDOULF   Is she a full grown woman?

RANDOULF 2   Woman noh interest yuh.

RANDOULF   I know, it's just a thought.

RANDOULF 2   Well don't taught about it any more.

RANDOULF   It was nothing deep.

RANDOULF 2   Shi brok bad… *(The bell rings)* Is who dat?

RANDOULF   Bloody hell. *(He creeps to the spy hole in the door.)*

RANDOULF 2   A bet is her man?

RANDOULF   It's only Nicole.

DOCTOR   It's lunch time, Randoulf…

RANDOULF 2   Don't answer it. Don't let her een. *(Randoulf indicates for him to be quiet)*

DOCTOR   Randoulf. *(He turns sharply)* It's time for lunch. *(He moves with urgency to quieten Randoulf 2)*

RANDOULF 2   Don't answer it. Don't let her een.

RANDOULF Shut up you fool. *(covering his mouth with his hand)* Be quiet. *(Nurse moves with syringe ready to use. Doctor indicates for him to stop)* I don't want to see her right now.

DOCTOR Randoulf! *(She startles him)* It's lunch-time.

RANDOULF She'll hear us.

DOCTOR There's no one there. (*moves to the door*)

RANDOULF Please don't. He won't like it.

DOCTOR *(opens the door for him to see)* See – there's no one here.

RANDOULF She's gone.

DOCTOR Yes. Now how about some lunch?

RANDOULF That's a good idea. *(He goes out.)*

DOCTOR Jesus Christ. He was on the loose? Thank god for prisons and institutions like these. *(Randoulf returns with lunch on a tray)* We'll continue after lunch.

RANDOULF I'm not going anywhere.

Exit Doctor and Nurse closing door behind them.

RANDOULF Enjoy your lunch Doctor. (*He puts half his lunch onto another plate*) In future, I'm not going to leave any more dinner for him. Every time, it's the same thing.
(*Enter Mother*)
I know he's late. Well there's no need to remind me. All right… from now on I won't cook for him… let him buy *Kentucky Fried Chicken* from The Colonel.
(*Enter Randoulf 2*)
You're late again. I'm just like a woman. This is the last time. I'm serious. Sit down. You're making the place

untidy. (*He pushes the chair out for him*) Every time I
prepare food, you're never around to enjoy it while it's
hot. Could you pass me the salt please? I'll get it myself. (*He gets it himself*) You find it hard to hand me the
salt. Yes you do. *Me* want *you* as a servant? You must
be joking. You eat like a pig. *(He stands and waters a
plant)* You stuff your face but you can't water these
beautiful green people. Where are you going? (*Randoulf
2 disappears*) Piss off you ungrateful–

Blackout.

SCENE 2
*Enter the Doctor looking around, followed by the Nurse
who stands by the door. Randoulf sits up sharply in bed.*

DOCTOR	Good afternoon, Randoulf.
RANDOULF	Good afternoon. *(He gets out of bed as*
if in the army)	
DOCTOR	How was lunch?
RANDOULF	Liver, boiled in water without any
marinade… as for the potatoes they were a bit on the	
hard side.	
DOCTOR	Don't exaggerate. It wasn't that bad.
RANDOULF	Really?
DOCTOR	I had the same. Believe it or not.
RANDOULF	And I'm your psychiatrist?
DOCTOR	The liver *was* dry without any marinade
and as for the potatoes, they could have been softer.	
RANDOULF	The mousse?
DOCTOR	An apple would have been kinder.
RANDOULF	You've really come to work, haven't
you Dr Kumar? *(She goes to speak)* Or to deceive me	
into friendship?	

DOCTOR   I'm getting to know you. As a person.

RANDOULF   My politeness has paid off but I'm worried about one thing...

DOCTOR   What is that Randoulf?

RANDOULF   I'm just praying that liver didn't come from a cow – like how I'm crazy already.

DOCTOR   Who said...?

RANDOULF   I've been labelled a violent paranoid schizophrenic.

DOCTOR   You're very tidy.

RANDOULF   I'm not interested in maids. I prefer to get my own hands dirty. *(He cleans up)* If you can't do something the right way – don't do it at all, as my mother used to say...

DOCTOR   Was your mother religious? *(No response)* We don't have to go there, if you find it uncomfortable.

RANDOULF   She believed in God.

DOCTOR   I sense some resentment.

RANDOULF   Cannot be helped. *(She turns on the tape-recorder)* The dictaphone to the rescue.

DOCTOR   Consistency matters.

RANDOULF   All women seem to speak alike.

DOCTOR   Really?

RANDOULF   That's what she said: "There's no escape from consistency or efficiency".

DOCTOR   She was a disciplinarian?

RANDOULF   That, as well. *(A beat)* She considered herself a black soul. She wanted to make it white. Angelic. She felt like she was being persecuted and as I matured, I felt the same.

DOCTOR   Would you say you and your mother suffer from delusions of persecution?

RANDOULF   If, feeling alienated and having other people's inadequacies dumped on me makes me suffer from *delusions* of being persecuted, then yes.

DOCTOR   Are you saying the hang-ups of... let's say people different from yourself, are handed to you and you take them on?

RANDOULF   Not only I but *we* take them on. We live our lives with all their deficiencies. For instance, my people truly dislike the texture of their hair.

DOCTOR   Some would consider these people fashionable.

RANDOULF   Fashion allows you to clean and groom yourself every day.

DOCTOR   I take it, you're referring to hair extensions?

RANDOULF   No. The dreaded weave. This human hair which black women wear belongs to dead people from under-developed countries, whose families have sold their scalp to pay for the funeral.

DOCTOR   Do you always generalise in such matters? *(A beat)* You don't like black people do you?

RANDOULF   I recognise the things that makes me feel ashamed of my own people. *(Long beat)* I recognise when I pass a brother in the street, a natural hatred creeps into my mind, violence seems to ooze from me towards him. That was one of the reasons I locked myself away... I didn't like those feelings – they where alien to me.

DOCTOR   That wasn't the only reason you locked yourself away, was it? *(Pause. She writes)* How long have you had this dislike for your own people?

RANDOULF   From as far back as I can remember ... *(A beat)* Since I've been here, I've had time to reflect. I'm ashamed of myself, of how I used to find the features of my race unattractive. We don't like our hair, we don't like our nose, we don't like our differences. We think our skin belongs to the devil. *(A beat)* Maybe that's why, it's so easy for us to kill each other?

DOCTOR That's truly how you see your people and yourself?

RANDOULF That's how *they* see us. We carry their burden, their inferior package about ourselves.

DOCTOR *(flicks back through papers)* Nicole – who was she?

RANDOULF She was a beautiful white lady. Blonde hair and blue eyes.

DOCTOR You're quite a character.

RANDOULF Or is that what you'd like me to be? Your kind of character?

DOCTOR *(studies him before she responds)* What kind of character would that be?

RANDOULF An obedient one?

DOCTOR You assume a lot.

RANDOULF *You* assume.

DOCTOR I assume to ask questions to reach and find answers.

RANDOULF So why don't you ask questions directly instead of – walking around London?

DOCTOR Then you wouldn't give me information about the middle ground.

RANDOULF You sound like a politician.

DOCTOR We're all politicians, one way or another.

RANDOULF Really?

DOCTOR Do you disagree?

RANDOULF Nicole was very interested in politics. If I'd listened to her, I wouldn't be here now…

DOCTOR You were saying?

RANDOULF Nicole was a very beautiful woman.

DOCTOR   So you said.

The bell rings. Randoulf 2 appears.

RANDOULF   Who is it?

RANDOULF 2   Is a woman, mek her tan out deh.

RANDOULF   Who is it? Is it *her* from downstairs?

RANDOULF 2 *(looks at him, stunned)* Noh, a di one who waan fuck yuh.

RANDOULF *(looks through the spy hole in the door)* Oh, it's Nicole.

RANDOULF 2   Woman noh good fi wi.

RANDOULF   It's not what you think.

RANDOULF 2   Open di door, mek her come een an mek wi si how much flesh shi hav pan display.

RANDOULF   You're so paranoid.

The Nurse moves to stop Randoulf, but the Doctor indicates to let him pass. He opens the door. Enter Nicole.

NICOLE   Randoulf, I wish I worked completely for myself, instead of some perverted up-start. *(helping herself to a drink)* You can never satisfy power mad people like him. *(She drinks)* God I needed that.

RANDOULF   Nicole. How are you?

NICOLE   I'm so frustrated.

RANDOULF 2   Si – shi start already.

RANDOULF   I know exactly how you feel. That's one of the reasons I prefer my own company.

RANDOULF 2   Tell her.

RANDOULF   I'm not including you… *(she moves closer)* …you know, what I mean.

NICOLE   Thank you. *(They hold each other)* Hug me tight, please.

RANDOULF 2   Don't dweet. *(Randoulf ignores this)*

NICOLE   I came to see you this morning but you were out.

RANDOULF   What time?

RANDOULF 2   Noh badder engage een meaningless conversation, it will lead toh seductive ones.

NICOLE   Around eleven.

RANDOULF   I had to meet someone in town, for eleven. Let me take your coat.

RANDOULF 2   Yuh fucking liar.

NICOLE   Hold this for me, please. *(She hands him her drink and takes off her coat)* Thank you. *(He hangs it up)* Drink with me… only depressed people drink alone.

RANDOULF 2   Shi need drink fi tell yuh seh shi waan fuck yuh. *(He moves behind the Doctor to hide from Randoulf)*

RANDOULF   Why don't you just piss off. *(The Doctor and Nicole exchange places)* Yes it is depressing to drink alone.

RANDOULF 2   Wha sweet nanny goat a goh run im belly.

RANDOULF *(fills his glass)* Cheers.

NICOLE   Cheers!

RANDOULF 2   Turn toh Gad buddy nat toh woman. They will mek yuh realise yuh juss a man.

NICOLE *(taking papers out of portfolio case)* I almost forgot why I was so frustrated earlier. The bastard wants you to make the characters blacker as well as the red redder.

RANDOULF   They're not happy?

NICOLE   Should we look at the story board?

RANDOULF 2   Shi come fi wok. *(He sits)*

RANDOULF   Now?

NICOLE   I just want to show you the areas which they're unhappy with. We need to look at level three, five and eight. *(He flicks to level three)*

RANDOULF   What's the problem here?

NICOLE   Here the blood is... too solid as he put it. *(She moves closer)*

RANDOULF   Level five?

NICOLE   Combination of the two... as he empties his gun, his complexion is too light. *(She holds his hand)* I like the original. Can you not alter this one? *(He nods)*

RANDOULF   Level eight? *(She finds it)*

NICOLE   Here the contrast of black skin and red blood is stunning to see... as the violence erupts... in other words, the shadow here should be the same shade as their skin.

RANDOULF   That's no problem. If that's what they want, that's what they shall have.

NICOLE   That's that. *(She brushes his cheek)*

RANDOULF 2   Careful. *(puts his arm around her. Gets up sharply)* A weh di rass a gwan ya?

RANDOULF   Sorry... *(pulls away)* ...I can't do this.

NICOLE   Why?

RANDOULF 2   Because yuh don't look like im people.

RANDOULF   Piss off. *(pretends to sneeze)*

NICOLE   Bless you.

RANDOULF   Thank you. *(goes to the window)*

NICOLE   She a friend?

RANDOULF   No.

NICOLE   She looks at you, like you owe her money.

RANDOULF   She lives downstairs… it's the first time we've seen one another.

RANDOULF 2   Liar.

RANDOULF   I hear him… *(He lowers his voice)* I hear him beating her up all the time.

NICOLE   Who?

RANDOULF   Her partner. *(She holds his arm)*

NICOLE   It's not surprising she looks at you in that manner.

RANDOULF 2   A give up.

NICOLE   She's embarrassed.

RANDOULF   Who?

NICOLE   *She* is.

RANDOULF   They're strange or should I say, *he* is… *(He looks around)* One moment he's beating her, the next they're at it, while she's screaming for the help of Christ. *(She moves away)*

RANDOULF 2   Gwan, tell her di woman business.

NICOLE   Can we change the subject?

RANDOULF 2   Mummy yuh cyaan seh yuh nevah try.

RANDOULF   Then they laugh like children.

NICOLE   Randoulf…

RANDOULF   Don't you think it's weird?

RANDOULF 2   Shi si yuh een aal yuh glory.

NICOLE   What about me and you?

RANDOULF 2   Her ears hard een?

RANDOULF   I'm cooking… would you like to stay and eat with me?

NICOLE   Stop changing the subject every time I corner you!

RANDOULF 2   Do nat sit een di council aaf di ungodly.

RANDOULF   Get out then!

NICOLE   I beg your pardon?

RANDOULF   Nicole... *(moves closer but Randoulf 2 pokes him when she touches him)*

NICOLE   Can't you drop your guard for once?

RANDOULF 2   Noh.

NICOLE   Sometimes I think you're afraid of me.

RANDOULF   Another drink?

NICOLE   I'd better be going.

We hear voices from off-stage.

JOSEPHINE   I don't feel ya blows anymore!

JULIAN   You're not going to any girls' night out. I'll kill ya first!

JOSEPHINE   Go on then kill me!

JULIAN   I said, you're not going anywhere.

JOSEPHINE   I'm not a pet Julian.

JULIAN   I'll use this.

JOSEPHINE   Cut me then... then what?

JULIAN   You've got too much fucking mouth... that's what's wrong wiv you.

JOSEPHINE   I wonder where I get it from?

JULIAN   Why do you always talk back to me? Why can't you just shut up?

JOSEPHINE   Go on. Cut me then!

JULIAN   You know I didn't mean it.

JOSEPHINE   Take your hands off me! Take them off!

JULIAN   A won't hit ya anymore.

JOSEPHINE   Let go of me.

JULIAN   Okay, okay. Sorry, Joe... I'll change.

JOSEPHINE   You do and say the same thing, every time.

JULIAN   I can't help it... I love you.

JOSEPHINE   No you don't.

JULIAN   I *do.*

JOSEPHINE   Why?

JULIAN   I feel safe with you.

JOSEPHINE   That's all the more reason why you should–

JULIAN   I don't like it when other men look at you... I'm frightened you're gonna run off...

JOSEPHINE   I wouldn't do that, I'm not like Aphelia.

JULIAN   I know.

JOSEPHINE   Really?

JULIAN   Yes.

JOSEPHINE   I'm frightened to put the key in the front door... I'm a bag of nerves – it's like walking on land mines.

JULIAN   I said I'm sorry!

JOSEPHINE   You have no respect for my body.

JULIAN   I do.

JOSEPHINE   Then why force me to have sex with you?

JULIAN   It's... it's just sometimes the feeling gets stronger...

JOSEPHINE   You, you, you, you, you! Now I see why black women turn to white men.

JULIAN   You what? *(He grabs her)* You think they don't beat their women as well?

JOSEPHINE   Get off! Arrrhh! Julian, no!

The sound of a struggle off-stage.

RANDOULF *(awkward)* They're at it again.

NICOLE   Don't you think we should go down and help?

RANDOULF   They'll make up any second now.

RANDOULF 2   Shi deserve everyting shi get.

RANDOULF   How she puts up with him for so long is criminal.

RANDOULF 2   A like shi like it.

RANDOULF   You honestly believe she enjoys a punch in the face?

RANDOULF 2   Yes.

NICOLE   Of course not... he must feed something in her.

RANDOULF 2   Siit deh... even shi cyaan siit.

RANDOULF   You're the only one who's witnessed their goings on with me. *(She puts her arm around him)*

RANDOULF 2   Apart fram mi. *(He indicates for Randoulf to back off)* Don't mek her get close to yuh again.

NICOLE   Don't you like women?

RANDOULF   Yes.

NICOLE   What's wrong with me?

RANDOULF 2   Everyting.

RANDOULF   I... I'm just not ready for a woman in my life.

RANDOULF 2   A could nat hav put it betta miself.

RANDOULF   I'm looking for a cold relationship.

NICOLE   Or is it that *my* complexion is unsuitable like the one in the game?

RANDOULF 2   Tell her di truth.

RANDOULF   Shut up!

NICOLE   Don't speak to me like that Randoulf.

RANDOULF   I was talking to myself. Nicole I/

RANDOULF 2   Wi/

RANDOULF   ...don't want to get emotionally involved with any woman. It's nothing to do with you.

NICOLE	I don't believe you.
RANDOULF 2	Tell her fi fuck aaf.
RANDOULF	It's true. *(She moves closer)*
NICOLE	Touch me.
RANDOULF *on her face)*	Nicole... *(She takes his hand and puts it*
RANDOULF 2 Stap it!	Don't allow her fi doh dat! *(He lets her)*
NICOLE	See, I'm real.
RANDOULF 2 Stap it!	Tell her fi come out! Oh Gad, noh!
NICOLE	I'm a woman and you're a man...

(He touches her face and body)

RANDOULF 2   Tek yuh han aaf her! A don't like dis at aal. A don't like it! A said a don't like it. A don't like it!

NICOLE	What do you see when you look at me?
RANDOULF	I see...
RANDOULF 2	Jesus Christ! Stap it!
RANDOULF	I see... *(Randoulf 2 moves in)*
RANDOULF 2 unity.	Tell her weh yuh si een na yuh comm-

RANDOULF   I see my women dropping their children at school... half an hour later, they're opening their garden to the infected agents...

NICOLE   When you look at *me,* is that what you see?

RANDOULF 2   Yes!

RANDOULF   I see people who call themselves Rasta-farians, who want nothing to do with England, walking into Sainsbury's, to buy their provisions. They can't even open their own shops to sell, yam, banana, okra and dasheen... the only religious group not to cater for themselves with a wealth of knowledge about herbs and medicines handed down to them by mothers and

grandmothers but they don't use it...
(Nicole gets her bag and coat)
Whenever *we* fight for equality, everybody jumps on the
bandwagon and benefits...

She exits, without Randoulf noticing.

RANDOULF 2   Shi gwan!

RANDOULF   Like Stephen Lawrence, whose death
will benefit all those lazy bastards who never fought for
anything decent in their lives.

RANDOULF 2   Shi gwan. Shi gwan. shi gwan, shi
gwan, shi gwan. *(He dances to his own rhythm)*

RANDOULF   God bless his mother and father for
giving birth to him again.

RANDOULF 2   Shi gwan. Shi gwan. Shi gwan, shi
gwan, shi gwan. *(skips round the room like a child)*

RANDOULF   We're having babies and dumping them
in telephone boxes...

RANDOULF 2 *(jumps on Randoulf)* Alright man yuh
cyaan tap-i now.

RANDOULF   How can I look upto women like these?

RANDOULF 2   Yuh cyaan, figet dem an seek Gad.
Spiritual satisfaction is wha yuh need... nat physical.

RANDOULF   As for our men...

RANDOULF 2   Yuh cyaan tap it now, shi gwan.

RANDOULF   They bark at them in the streets like
dogs. As for our musicians... some of the lyrics they
come up with – you'd think they were talking about
mutations of science. They wear garments that ride up
their arses to sell records... *(Randoulf 2 jumps off him)*
Do you understand Nicole? Nicole...

RANDOULF 2   Randoulf shi an wi different.

RANDOULF   She should understand...

RANDOULF 2   Woman noh understand everyting.

RANDOULF   She's really gone?

RANDOULF 2   Yes. Now aal di woman out-ta di way. Wi cyaan worship Gad full time. *(sits and puts his feet on the table)* Mek us both a drink, wi wok hard toh deh.

RANDOULF   We must alleviate the suffering of women. We must walk the streets and entice the most complicated, down- trodden woman and lavish her with every loving emotion mummy never had.

RANDOULF 2   Stap tark fart an mek di drink dem.

RANDOULF *(pours a drink)* And I would want nothing in return… only to see a stress-free woman without any pain or hostility.

The bell rings.

RANDOULF 2   Oh yuh finish yuh trip aaf nostalgia? About time toh, a was dying fi watta.

DOCTOR   For the record, the patient was in a transient state and was physically violent and aggressive in language. But it must be noted the patient was and is unaware of his transformation.

RANDOULF 2   A wish yuh would stap caaling mummy name een vain, everyting yuh doh yuh hav her een mine. Tanks. *(He drinks)* Dere's noting like ice watta. Praise di lard. Seh it.

RANDOULF   What?

RANDOULF 2   Praise di lard, seh it.

RANDOULF   Praise the lord.

RANDOULF 2   Amen.

RANDOULF   Amen.

RANDOULF 2   A going out. *(He turns)* Fram now arn, every time wi eat, wi ha fi seh prayers as well as bed time, right? Een fack mek wi kneel. *(He kneels)* Weh

yuh a wait fa? Prostrate een front a di lard. *(Randoulf
kneels)* Seh aafta mi.

RANDOULF   Is this warranted?

RANDOULF 2   Weh yuh mean warrented? Yuh tink
yuh a police?

RANDOULF   No.

RANDOULF 2   Den shut yuh mout den. Repeat aafta
mi. Dear Mummy...

RANDOULF   Dear Mummy...

RANDOULF 2   Tank yuh fi nat aborting us.

RANDOULF   Thank you for not aborting us.

RANDOULF 2   An fi breast feeding wi pan yuh natural
nutriments.

RANDOULF *(peeks a look)* And... for breast-feeding us
on your natural nutriments.

RANDOULF 2   Wi appreciate di pain yuh goh trew wid
dat violent bastard.

RANDOULF   We appreciate the pain you went though
with that violent bastard.

RANDOULF 2   Who nevah hav any consideration fi yuh
insides.

RANDOULF   Who had no consideration for your
insides whatsoever.

RANDOULF 2   Nat figetting di pain wi cause yuh een di
delivery-room because aaf wi big head.

RANDOULF *(half-protests)* Not forgetting the pain we
caused you in the delivery-room because of his big
head.

RANDOULF 2   Fi wi.

RANDOULF   Our big head.

RANDOULF 2   Amen.

RANDOULF   Amen

RANDOULF 2   Si yuh late-ta.

RANDOULF   What time?

DOCTOR   Exercise time.

RANDOULF   Exercise time?

DOCTOR   Yes, exercise. *(He looks up at the Doctor and for the first time is aware that he's on his knees)*

RANDOULF   I'd like to be left... alone.

DOCTOR   Exercise is compulsory. *(Randoulf pulls himself together and exits with the Nurse)*
Second session terminated at fifteen forty-five.
Randoulf is displaying paranoid symptoms towards his mother, women generally, as well as his inner self. His mother has been a major influence on his mind. I'm not sure if women are as important to him, as he believes. The patient personality appears to be split and for the first time religion has entered the assessment, in the form of prayer. In prayer he believes he prolonged the labour of his mother in childbirth, inflicting unnecessary pain, because his head was too big. He also seems to think that his father was violent and without consideration for his mother... *(Nurse enters)*
I just find him fascinating. Can you imagine putting your ear to a glass and hearing other people's conversations?

NURSE *(stops at the door and looks back)* Are you coming?

DOCTOR   I'll be there shortly.

Lights fade down slowly.

SCENE 3
Randoulf's cell door has been left open. We see a long corridor leading from his cell door. Two male guards escort him to his cell.

RANDOULF   In here, it's as cold as a fridge and it's summer outside. In here, they'll do anything to disturb your balance. The guy who designed this place – credit is due to him, he's used concrete like a magician.

GUARD 1   Randoulf... this is all in your mind, like most things. Do you think I'm wearing a t- shirt because it's winter?

RANDOULF   You're part of it. Everybody else knows it but refuses to say anything.

GUARD 1   Shut up you schizo.

RANDOULF   Same to you.

GUARD 1 *(slams the door)* Hay Harry, he finks it's winta.

GUARD 2   Go along wiv him Pete, it's easier.

GUARD 1   You know why that is, don't ya?

GUARD 2   No.

GUARD 1   This fucker was first sectioned in February.

GUARD 2   Poor bastard, he must live in a time warp.

The Doctor approaches.

GUARD 1   Good afternoon, Dr Kumar.

DOCTOR   Good afternoon, officers.

GUARD 1   Please allow me to do that for you. *(He unlocks the door)*

DOCTOR   Thank you.

GUARD 1   Just ring if you need any assistance.

DOCTOR   I don't think that will be necessary but if the occasion does arise... *(She finds Randoulf sitting on his bed, wrapped in his blanket.)* Good afternoon Randoulf, how was exercise?

RANDOULF   Fine until I entered the interior.

DOCTOR   Are you ill?

RANDOULF   Just cold.

DOCTOR   It's seventy outside.

RANDOULF   It's amazing how concrete allows you to appreciate the sun.

DOCTOR   Are you sure you haven't got a fever?

RANDOULF *(snapping)* I'm fine, thank you very much, just cold.

DOCTOR   Sorry, for being considerate.

RANDOULF   What is this?... Pick on Randoulf week?

DOCTOR   What happened while you were out on exercise?

RANDOULF   If you must know, *it* called me a paranoid schizophrenic.

DOCTOR   Who?

RANDOULF   That... *(moves to the door with the blanket)* ... under-nourished thing.

DOCTOR   It's just jolly banter.

RANDOULF   We're all growing an unusual sense of humour.

DOCTOR   I'll give him a ticking off later. Now can we get back to business?

RANDOULF   I'm just a job to you?

DOCTOR   And an interesting job at that. *(taking out tape-recorder and file)* Where were we?

RANDOULF   Shouldn't you turn that on first? *(She turns on tape recorder)* After all, I might flip my lid and turn into a paranoid schizophrenic. *(She flicks latch on the door, for a quick exit.)*

DOCTOR   This will be sufficient. *(Pause)* So you're shaped by what you see and hear?

RANDOULF   Where's your minder? *(moving away)*

DOCTOR   I'm here to work with you. *(She walks nervously into centre of room)*

RANDOULF   Why? *(He stares at her)*

DOCTOR   I need to help. *(uncomfortable)*

RANDOULF   You need to help *me*? *(He lets the blanket drop to the floor)*

DOCTOR   Yes. *(He moves closer to tape recorder)* So you're shaped by what you see and hear?

RANDOULF   If I wasn't, then I'd be a milk bottle. *(He turns off tape recorder)* You're taking a risk Doctor... very unprofessional.

DOCTOR   Elasticised rules work better. *(She turns it back on)*

RANDOULF   You obviously have plans for me.

DOCTOR   Professional ones, yes. *(He studies her)* It seems Nicole didn't take your political rhetoric lightly?

RANDOULF   You have been listening.

DOCTOR   Did you cross boundaries?

RANDOULF   What boundaries?

DOCTOR   The racial one. *(A beat)*

RANDOULF   No. My mother's teachings would never allow it. *(He picks up blanket and begins to make the bed)*

DOCTOR   She's a very powerful woman, your mother.

RANDOULF   Weak mothers nurture weak children.

DOCTOR   So you were never intimate with Nicole? Even though the feelings were strong?

RANDOULF   This is not my country, politically.

DOCTOR   Did you fall to temptation? *(A beat)*

RANDOULF   Doctor Shipman has been found guilty.

DOCTOR   You *did,* didn't you?

RANDOULF   He has abused the power a patient gives to a Doctor.

DOCTOR   We're all allowed to be weak...

RANDOULF *(turns to face her)* I did *not* fall to temptation! I – yes I, have enough discipline to go around, unlike the majority of people who walk the face of this earth! You! You could never walk the hills and gullies I have climbed. You would stay down at the first obstacle.

DOCTOR   Why didn't you?

RANDOULF   Because she's white and I'm black.

DOCTOR   So what?

RANDOULF   So *what?*

DOCTOR   It's not like she's a spider and you're a whale. *(Pause)*

RANDOULF   I love the aloe vera plant, I had six of them once. When attention wasn't paid to them, they'd wither, but give them a good drink and how they firmed up. Their flesh was like muscle – soft and elastic, as well as exciting to touch. *(He strokes the Doctor)* How good is your man in bed?

DOCTOR   None of your business.

RANDOULF   What colour is he? Black, White... Indian, Arab, Chinese?

DOCTOR   He's a man and that's all you need to know.

RANDOULF *(grabs her and pulls her to him)* I can do a passionate job for you. *(She slaps him.)*

DOCTOR *(Long beat)* Look what you made me do.

RANDOULF   I can see you in the closet and you're violent.

DOCTOR   We need a break. *(walks towards the door)*

RANDOULF   I'd like to take you on another trip, before you end this session, if you'd allow me.

DOCTOR *(turns)* Please do.

RANDOULF   Do you know Ajiboha in room X?

DOCTOR   I know her.

RANDOULF   Beautiful woman, shapely and well-educated. She's from Nigeria, right? *(She nods)* Doesn't believe a woman should wait on a man but fell in love with a Nigerian career man, so her studying began to falter. Then she fell pregnant while taking the pill and thought his family were casting spells against her. So secretly, she aborted their child... stopped plaiting her hair, painted her lips the reddest red she could find... and now when she walks past black men, there's this disgusted look on her face... You remind me of her.

DOCTOR   Really, why?

RANDOULF   It's hard for black women and men. Any one of us could end up in one of these five star hotels, including you.

DOCTOR   I very much doubt that.

RANDOULF   Sectioning a race of people just because they believe in different things, is sinful.

DOCTOR   Thou shall not kill. *(Long beat)*

RANDOULF   I knew you could play dirty.

DOCTOR   Let's pretend I never uttered those words.

RANDOULF   No I want to keep them. Sin never lets you off the hook... it eats away at you continually. You don't under-stand do you...? *(She turns to leave)* That's right – run, but before you go let me explain it to you in another way. *(She stops)* Take a dog for instance... remove it from its pack, place it in a middle-class home, eventually it will start to change and behave like a human... Now it only looks like a dog. When it meets another dog, it fights, instead of figuring a way to get the noose from around its neck. This tame dog meets an angry bull-mastiff who bites back and in a dog's world once you bite your master they put you down.

DOCTOR   You see black people as the bull-mastiffs who are being put down? *(He claps her)*

RANDOULF   And when we bite... they say, see we told you so.

DOCTOR   We can all avoid bites.

RANDOULF   I have noticed.

DOCTOR   We'll finish this later.

RANDOULF   Julian had a dog. *(He turns and walks away)* He bought it knowing full well she was terrified of dogs. He would talk to it as if it were a woman, asking it to pose for pictures. At one time I thought it was a bit on the side.

We hear the sound of a dog barking and screams from off-stage. Randoulf 2 appears. Randoulf puts his ear to the floor.

RANDOULF 2   Now wi narh goh get noh sleep ti-night.

RANDOULF   Did you hear that?

RANDOULF 2   Hear wha?

RANDOULF   She's screaming again.

RANDOULF 2   Dat's weh shi doh aal di time.

RANDOULF   No. Listen. *(They listen)*

RANDOULF 2   Mi cyann hear anyting.

RANDOULF   Shh! *(More barking)*

JOSEPHINE   Julian, get him away from me.

JULIAN   Sic her. *(Barking)*

JOSEPHINE   Don't let him go! Please, please.

JULIAN   Stay still or I'll let him go.

JOSEPHINE   Alright Julian, alright!

JULIAN   Heel boy. Panasonic, sit. Come and stroke him.

JOSEPHINE   Julian, no.

JULIAN	Panasonic. *(Barking)*
JOSEPHINE	Alright!... I'll stroke him.... Oh Julian please.
JULIAN	Stroke him.
JOSEPHINE	Make him sit.

JULIAN   Sit boy. Good boy... good boy. See that wasn't bad was it? You see, Joe I bought him so you'll never leave me.

JOSEPHINE   I'd never leave you.

JULIAN   He's my right hand man. When I'm not here he'll be on guard. Only I'll feed him, not you.

JOSEPHINE   He'll bite me when you're not here.

JULIAN   I'll feed him plenty.

RANDOULF 2   But wait im really sick.

RANDOULF   Sick? He's a flipping nutter.

RANDOULF 2   Bwoy im muss si really love her. *(They listen)*

JULIAN   I'll train him to walk behind you anywhere you go. *(Barking)* Shut up. Sit. I don't want you to phone any of your so-called friends anymore and you only go out when it's completely necessary. Got it?

JOSEPHINE   Yes.

JULIAN   Another thing... I don't want you phoning any of your relatives and to make sure you don't I'll be taking the phones with me every time I leave.

JOSEPHINE   Julian...

JULIAN   Do I make myself clear?

RANDOULF 2   How somma dem woman ask man fi come live wid dem an dem noh know noting bout dem. Wha ever im gi her im waan somting back een return, shi muss hav one big ego.

RANDOULF   That could happen to anybody. They show you what they want you to see and when they have you they give you the real character.

RANDOULF 2   Nat like mi an yuh ha? Up front wid noh apologies. But dem noh waan people like mi an yuh.

RANDOULF   You know sometimes you're right. Our own company is best.

RANDOULF 2   If A don't look out fi yuh an yuh don't look out fi mi, who a goh look out fi wi?

RANDOULF   Yes, we are important... *(The bell rings)* Who the hell is that?

RANDOULF 2   Answer di door an yuh will fine out. *(The bell rings. Randoulf looks through the spy hole)*

RANDOULF   It's Nicole... what's she doing back here?

RANDOULF 2   A wonder if her baggie hav anyting fi doh wid it.

Enter Nicole.

NICOLE   Sorry for walking out on you the other day.

RANDOULF   I was the insensitive one. *(He hugs her)*

RANDOULF 2   Yuh lucky yuh narh doh noting crooked, carr shi would da surely tark.

NICOLE   I'm not staying long. How are the adjustments going?

RANDOULF   Nearly there and *Domestics* is finished.

NICOLE   Great.

RANDOULF   Would you like a drink?

NICOLE   A glass of water please.

RANDOULF 2   Mi sure shi waan somting strangga dan dat.

RANDOULF   Coming up.

NICOLE   This one is going to be a monster.

RANDOULF   I hope so… a lot of work has gone into it.

NICOLE   Thank you.

RANDOULF   Still friends? *(She nods)*

RANDOULF 2   Nat if A cyaan help it.

RANDOULF   Shut up. *(under his breath)*

NICOLE   I was –

RANDOULF   Thinking out loud… please continue.

NICOLE   Sometimes I wish I was the same colour as you.

RANDOULF 2   Shi hav di same complex as fi wi women.

RANDOULF   Nicole…

NICOLE   Just to see if you'd at least be tempted.

RANDOULF   I am tempted.

RANDOULF 2   Weh di rass yuh goh tell her dat fa? Wi marrid toh Gad aready.

NICOLE   Do you want children? Just curious.

RANDOULF 2   Done di conversation now.

NICOLE   One day you're going to love and it's going to hurt.

RANDOULF 2   Nevah.

NICOLE   The women you want will top you up with pain every time they see love on your face.

RANDOULF 2   Wi responsible. Love, jealousy an possession. *(They say together-)*

RANDOULF   I've no time for such primitive passions.

NICOLE   Talking to yourself again? You're on the verge of madness and unaware of it. *(Randoulf laughs)*

RANDOULF 2   Laugh again, buddy. *(He does)*

NICOLE   If you had more visitors they'd see the same thing.

RANDOULF 2 *(moves in between them)* Discretion, dis
one is an observer.

NICOLE Maybe if you had more female company... Are you capable of loving? *(A beat)*

RANDOULF 2 Gad is who im love.

NICOLE It's true what they say...

RANDOULF Who?

NICOLE Women in love. *(He walks away)* When
true love is in front of a man, he never sees it...

RANDOULF I'd still like us to remain friends.

NICOLE *(gets her coat and bag)* So we shall.

She leaves.

RANDOULF 2 Weh shi expeck anyway?

RANDOULF You make ice feel warm.

RANDOULF 2 Fram yuh honest wid people, dem hav fi
respeck yuh. Anyway yuh hav enough pan yuh plate
aready.

RANDOULF I need a drink.

RANDOULF 2 A bet yuh could doh wid a rum? *(He
jumps into his arms)*

RANDOULF Yes.

RANDOULF 2 Don't touch di fire watta, drink watta dat
our Lard has produced fi wi.

The bell rings.

DOCTOR Randoulf.

RANDOULF What!

RANDOULF 2 Dat is why wi couldn't touch her, shi a
noh di right one.

RANDOULF   I should be allowed to forn... forni... fornicate! *(Randoulf 2 stares at him)* At least once a month.

RANDOULF 2   Tek it easy. *(He fights Randoulf at a distance. The Doctor watches in amazement)* Yuh know seh mi trang-ga dan yuh.

RANDOULF   Ever since I allowed you to converse with me, you've taken over and dominated my life and I don't like it. *(They continue to fight)* Get off! Get off! Get off!
(The Doctor places her hand on his chest to bring him round. Randoulf 2 lets go and disappears)
I told you to let go of me. Let go. *(He relaxes)*

DOCTOR   I did Randoulf, as soon as I realised I was hurting you.

RANDOULF *(lying on the floor)* You should have let go of me sooner.

DOCTOR *(backing off)* There was a little complication or I would have let you go sooner.

RANDOULF   Don't you ever pin me down like that again.

DOCTOR   I won't do it again.

RANDOULF   I want to be alone.

DOCTOR   I understand. *(She backs out of the room)*

Blackout.

ACT TWO
SCENE 1
Young Randoulf is sitting at the table drinking a glass of water. He watches his mother cleaning and cooking. As she is preparing the food she calls him over and talks to him.

MOTHER   Do you see how hard I have to work Randoulf? *(He shakes his head)* That's because I'm on my own. That wasn't the way I wanted to spend the prime of my life. *(She gives him a piece of carrot)* Do you love me Randoulf?

YOUNG RANDOULF Yes, mummy. *(with his mouth full)*

MOTHER   Don't talk with your mouth full. *(He nods)* I love you... it would have been nice to have your father loving you too. Yuh want anadda piece? *(He nods)* I want you to be able to look after yourself, to watch me cook and help me to prepare the food.

YOUNG RANDOULF I thought only women cooked food.

MOTHER   Everybody cooks if they know what's good for them. *(She gives him a carrot to cut up)*

YOUNG RANDOULF Can I?

MOTHER   Carefully hold the carrot like this... *(She shows him)* and you won't cut your fingers. Understand?

YOUNG RANDOULF I think so. *(He copies her)* I can do it. *(He smiles)*

MOTHER   Keep your eyes on the knife at all times. If you cut yourself, it's not the knife's fault. *(She turns his head)* This way, you'll keep all your fingers. *(She watches him do it, proudly)*

YOUNG RANDOULF I like cooking.

MOTHER *(laughs)* This is preparing.

YOUNG RANDOULF What is preparing Mummy?

MOTHER *(kisses the top of his head)* Detail.

YOUNG RANDOULF What's detail?

MOTHER   It's a way of finding out if the opposite sex is suitable for you... if they were reared properly. Good hygiene, manners, courtesy etc.

YOUNG RANDOULF Mummy, will I get to know all these things?

MOTHER   Gard spear mi life... and if he does, I'll equip you with them all. Now go and set the table. Your dinner's nearly ready. *(He makes to protest. She kisses him affectionately)* You'll be saying prayers this evening.

The Doctor enters with caution. Randoulf is lost in his memories. The Mother and Young Randoulf disappear.

DOCTOR   Is everything fine? *(No response from Randoulf)* Randoulf? *(Randoulf 2 appears)*

RANDOULF 2   A tek it yuh an Nicole noh si eye toh eye anymore? *(No response)* Wi tark di truth.

RANDOULF   I have given her a set of keys to cushion the blow.

RANDOULF 2   Why?

RANDOULF   She means well.

RANDOULF 2   Now shi cyaan wark een pan wi any time.

RANDOULF   Maybe that's exactly what I want... I might even invite the one and a half friends I have left, thanks to you.

RANDOULF 2   Buddy, dem kinna woman don't like independent man, like wi.

RANDOULF   Shut up!

RANDOULF 2   Dem waan wi fi depen pan dem fi everyting. Mummy doh her job well, very well eendeed but dat deh woman is nat fi yuh. *(Randoulf sits next to the Doctor)* Let us pray... come noh. *(He kneels)* Oh lard tank yuh fi giing us di spirit aaf how-wa madder, Gi her strength soh dat her sprit conquer an beat dong di drugs giing toh her fi experiment. *(He pulls Randoulf down* *too)* Mek her know once again wi hav been tempted an wi conquered di beast an pass di test wid flying colours.

RANDOULF Aaaaamen.

RANDOULF 2 And Fardda has as fram tohdeh, wi are married toh yuh an noh woman shall ever again fornicate wid us. Amen.

RANDOULF *(reluctantly)* Amen.

RANDOULF 2 Yuh cyaan tan up now. *(He stands)* Weh yuh gi her di key fa?

RANDOULF I don't want to lose her as a friend. It was embarrassing while she was here, to hear those screams coming from that woman...

RANDOULF 2 Yuh cyann help every baddy. Yuh need help toh.

RANDOULF I am self-sufficient, mummy made sure of that.*(Barking can be heard again)* She's unhappy again.

RANDOULF 2 Put arn some music.

RANDOULF No... He's gone out and left her with the dog. *(The sound of doors being slammed)* She's out the front door... *(He goes to the window)* She's terrified. Look at her.

RANDOULF 2 Mi noh interested in shi meking.

RANDOULF She's seen me again. She must think I'm a right pervert.

RANDOULF 2 Weh shi a goh tink yuh a pervert fa?

RANDOULF I have no woman.

RANDOULF 2 Yuh worry bout her man.

RANDOULF I don't worry... *(The bell rings)* Who can that be?

RANDOULF 2 Guess who? *(He lays on the bed)* If a shi, shi know yuh deh ya.

RANDOULF What if it's him? *(He creeps to the door)*

RANDOULF 2 Den yuh betta harm yuhself.

RANDOULF *(whispers)* It's her.

RANDOULF 2   Si yuh chance ya fi doh di tings superman cyann doh, een real life, save a woman een distress. *(He jumps off bed)* Wi don't need saarf flesh seh it.

RANDOULF   We don't need soft flesh.

RANDOULF 2   Because wi love Gad.

Josephine enters uninvited.

JOSEPHINE   Sorry to bother you... but I need help. He and that dog gonna kill me.

RANDOULF   I don't want to get involved in other people's arguments.

JOSEPHINE   You won't. Just somewhere safe for five minutes.

RANDOULF   I...

JOSEPHINE *(accusingly)* I know you know he beats me.

RANDOULF   Calm down, calm down.

RANDOULF 2   As soon as yuh touch her, yuh hook.

JOSEPHINE   The dog… the dog watches over me all the time. I can't take it anymore.

RANDOULF   If you'd like to use my phone…

JOSEPHINE   The police don't listen and if they do my other fight is with the judges… He knows all my friends… where they live...

RANDOULF   Would you like a drink? Tea or coffee?

JOSEPHINE   A large brandy would be better, please.

RANDOULF   Ice?

RANDOULF 2   Da woman deh, shi noh respect Gad ar ` man, shi wi cuss Christ aaf di crass.

JOSEPHINE   No thanks. You won't say anything, will you?

RANDOULF   Do I look crazy to you? For godsakes get away from the window.

JOSEPHINE   Promise me you won't say anything. Promise me.

RANDOULF   I promise. *(A beat)* Drink this, it might help you to relax.

JOSEPHINE   Sorry for being so... thank you. I'm alright. Could I use your toilet?

RANDOULF   Through there, turn left. *(She goes out)*

Lights change.

DOCTOR   Did Josephine go home that night? *(He comes around)* Did she go home that night?

RANDOULF   Yes. *She* moved my spirit. *He* didn't like it. *He* didn't like the way we were being moved. *She* began to cry. I did all I could to make her feel safe but still the tears came seeping out. *She* didn't know who she was any more... Do you know something, Doctor?

DOCTOR   Rani. *(A beat)*

RANDOULF   Most people think they know about this violence but to see it and hear it... is brutal.

DOCTOR   Elaborate. *(She studies him)*

RANDOULF   Her eyes would go wild as if death was about to claim her... normal movements from me would frighten her... her nerves had gone... she wished she was a man so she could kill him.

DOCTOR   She wished she was a man?

RANDOULF   If she was a man she'd have a legal argument in the courts – provocation. *(She nods)* ... as soon as she got in, he beat her.

The sounds of an argument from off-stage.

JULIAN   Panasonic! *(Barking)*

JOSEPHINE   Julian... *(The sound of feet running)*
Help! Julian!

JULIAN   Scream one more time and I'll break
your face. Take your clothes off. *(To dog)* Shud up!

JOSEPHINE   Julian please, please. No.

RANDOULF   He's gonna kill her.

RANDOULF 2   If a noh one ting a di nex.

RANDOULF   What should I do?

RANDOULF 2   Mine yuh own business, dat's weh fi
doh.

RANDOULF   It's two against one.

RANDOULF 2   Fi gad sake. Dat beast im hav dong deh
mek two an im mek three?

RANDOULF   Everything is a joke to you.

RANDOULF 2   If A woz yuh A wouldn't mek her come
back up ya. Shi look like one a dem blood suck-ka

RANDOULF   They've stopped.

RANDOULF 2   Siit deh, is di same routine as aalways,
aal wi need now is di laugh-ta

RANDOULF   Maybe he's killed her.

RANDOULF 2   A waan im kill her soh wi cyaan get
some peace an quiet.

RANDOULF   I need to piss. *(He goes out)*

RANDOULF 2   Wi cyann sleep fi more dan a hour
widout dat cartoon caper disturbing us. *(He gets in the
bed)*

*The Doctor follows Randoulf out then returns and waits.
Randoulf returns and takes in where he is.*

RANDOULF   I feel tired.

DOCTOR   You've been talking for a long time. Would you like us to stop for a while?

RANDOULF   No... Where was I?

DOCTOR *(flicks through her notes)* ... maybe he's killed her. They were your last words.

RANDOULF   He was beating her up again, wasn't he? *(She nods. He smiles)* A few days later she invited herself to dinner.

DOCTOR   Did you love her?

RANDOULF   I told her... that was my first mistake.

The bell rings. Randoulf 2 sits up sharply. Randoulf jumps.

RANDOULF 2   Pussy rule di world bwoy. Wen pussy seh jump yuh jump.

RANDOULF *(awkward)* You... you look beautiful. Come in.

RANDOULF 2   If yuh a goh seh someting seh it convincingly.

Josephine enters.

JOSEPHINE   Thank you. *(She hands him a bottle of brandy)* For you, with appreciation.

RANDOULF   Remy – this is too much.

JOSEPHINE   I appreciate good things and I think you do too.

RANDOULF   I'm flattered.

RANDOULF 2   Hav aal di bull-shit.

JOSEPHINE   Don't I get a kiss? Well? *(He kisses her cheek)*

RANDOULF   Would you like ice?

RANDOULF 2   Shi cyann si yuh nat very good at dis. Mine yuh noh ejaculate pan yuhself before shi ready.

JOSEPHINE   Something smells nice.

RANDOULF 2   Cock-ki.

RANDOULF   Jamaican.

JOSEPHINE   You're a bachelor? Or are you?

RANDOULF   Yes, I wouldn't have it any other way.

RANDOULF 2   Yuh hav resistance aafta aal.

JOSEPHINE   You're a very tidy man. *(She walks around)* Are you sure there's no woman you pull out once in a while?

RANDOULF   No, this is the way I was brought up.

JOSEPHINE   Men like you frighten women.

RANDOULF 2   Except yuh.

RANDOULF   Do I frighten you?

JOSEPHINE   No… are you gay?

RANDOULF 2   Tell her yes.

RANDOULF   My mischievous mind tells me to give you some inclination that I am, but no, I'm not.

JOSEPHINE   Julian thinks you are.

RANDOULF   That's not a bad thing. Now I feel safer.

JOSEPHINE   Most men want to give the impression that they're fighters.

RANDOULF 2   Siit deh now. Aal dis unnecessary tark, juss tek aaf di woman baggie an gi her weh shi waan.

JOSEPHINE   You drink slow. *(filling his glass)*

RANDOULF   Sorry.

RANDOULF 2 *(sarcastic)* Sarry?

JOSEPHINE   You're so sweet.

RANDOULF 2   Look pan her. Look how shi a lick her lip dem, by di time shi finish wid yuh Kentucky narh seh noting.

JOSEPHINE   A change of company is a good thing. *(She kisses him)* ...Good treatment is so beautiful. *(He moves closer and spills her drink)* It doesn't matter...

RANDOULF   Sorry... I'll get you one of my shirts while yours...

JOSEPHINE   It's alright... it'll be fine. *(He gives her a shirt and goes out. She takes off her dress and examines her bruises in the mirror)* What I would give to be a man right now.

RANDOULF *(enters)* Oh, sorry. Jesus Christ!

RANDOULF 2   Yuh tink dat woz a accident?

JOSEPHINE   They're nothing... they're my second skin.

RANDOULF   I was wondering why you had no bruises on your face.

JOSEPHINE   The whole world would see he's beating me. This way they think that it's all in my head....

RANDOULF 2   Mi narh look pan dem noh more. *(He exits)*

JOSEPHINE   ... don't let it spoil our evening.

RANDOULF   I can't believe a strapping man like him would do this to a woman. It's not even a challenge.

JOSEPHINE   Please... you're getting angry and you're frightening me.

RANDOULF   Sorry... *(They kiss)*

JOSEPHINE   ...so gentle... I wish that kiss could make them go away.

RANDOULF   You're... you're still beautiful... *(A beat)* If he beats you, I feel the pain. If he makes love to you, I feel jealous. If you laugh together it hurts...

JOSEPHINE   How?

She turns the light out. Josephine disappears. Randoulf 2 returns, singing. Lights up slowly.

RANDOULF 2   Di first cut is the deepest… Weh yuh gi een fa? En? Weh… *(He follows Randoulf)* It woz obvious weh shi di waan!

RANDOULF   Shut up.

RANDOULF 2   Yuh tell mi noh more woman, right?

RANDOULF   Right.

RANDOULF 2   Noh more emotional involvement, right?

RANDOULF   Right.

RANDOULF 2   Soh why fuck wid her?

RANDOULF   I'm not emotionally involved.

RANDOULF 2   Who yuh fooling?

RANDOULF   It was just sex… that's all it was.

RANDOULF 2   Before lang shi wi hav yuh eating out ta one darg bowl. A don't waan yuh fi si her again. Promise mi.

RANDOULF   No!

RANDOULF 2   Shi wi put arn perfume until yuh nostrils pick her up in-na Portugal. *(Randoulf hides)* Shi will flirt until jealousy is di hallmark aaf yuh face. *(Randoulf is on the bed, hands over his ears)* Dat baddy? Yes, dat baddy. Shi will tone it toh perfection an yuh will believe shi woz especially mek fi yuh. Wen shi oil it… yes, sometimes wid yuh help, it will shine…

RANDOULF   What do you want me to do? Be like an old man in a young man's body?

RANDOULF 2   Di woman dangerous.

RANDOULF   Shut up! *(grabs for him and misses)*

RANDOULF 2   Shi a divide wi an is ruling yuh an yuh cyann siit.

RANDOULF *(goes to the door and holds it open)* Out, out, out, out, out! You're bad news!

RANDOULF 2   At least yuh know di news A bring. *(He goes)*

RANDOULF   Where you going?

RANDOULF 2   Yuh bline as well as stupid?

RANDOULF   Come back… the blood was hot.

RANDOULF 2   Mi goh deh aready wid yuh, mi narh goh back deh again. *(pushes him away)*

RANDOULF   Why can't I have friends you don't like and vice versa? *(grabs Randoulf 2 and spins him round to face him. Randoulf 2 pushes him back forcefully, then exits. He crawls after him.)* I said sorry! Alright… I took you for granted. Stay!… *(Pause)* You're just like the rest of them anyway… holding me back, telling all my secrets… You'll come back… they all do. I don't fucking need you anyway!

The Doctor creeps past him quietly and exits.
Blackout.

SCENE 2
Randoulf is sleeping in his bed. Enter Doctor with two silver trays of food, quietly setting the table for them both.

DOCTOR   Oh you're awake. Had a good sleep?

RANDOULF   How long have I been sleeping? *(gets up and makes the bed)*

DOCTOR   About two hours.

RANDOULF   I must have been extremely tired.

DOCTOR   Yes, something like that.

RANDOULF   I'm usually quite alert.

DOCTOR   I'd like to eat with you, if you don't mind.

RANDOULF   Why the hell do you want to come in this box and eat the same shit I eat? *(A beat.)*

DOCTOR   I hope you like what I chose... *(indicates a chair)*... for us... *(he walks over to the table)*...Which one would you prefer?

RANDOULF *(laughs)* You're working on me.

DOCTOR   I am assessing you, after all.

RANDOULF   What do you want or have you taken it already?

DOCTOR   Fish or chicken? I'm not used to eating cold food... the chef won't re-heat, for anyone.

RANDOULF   I think we should introduce the palate to both. *(A beat. She laughs)*

DOCTOR   Yes, I agree. *(She shares out the food)* Trust is a hard thing to come by and like you, I think people should work for it.

RANDOULF *(watching her every move)* You want my trust...? Why?

DOCTOR   We all need to trust sometimes.

RANDOULF   So people can take advantage of me?

DOCTOR   If Ranjha never loved Heer or Adam never loved Eve, we wouldn't have those wonderful stories... with all the passion that flowed in them... trust was the key... This is not bad at all.

RANDOULF *(swaps the dinners)* I wouldn't know. I haven't tasted it.

DOCTOR   Randoulf?

RANDOULF   Yes.

DOCTOR   This person that speaks to you... who is he? Or she?

RANDOULF *(taking knife and fork)* I'm glad you like it. I'll give the chef your personal approval.

DOCTOR   ...your friend who's always around.

RANDOULF   He doesn't trust anybody but himself.

DOCTOR   Not even you?

RANDOULF   Not even me.

DOCTOR   Do *you* trust *him*?

RANDOULF   Once upon a time I did.

DOCTOR   What changed?

RANDOULF   He controlled me and he was a jealous god. *(A long beat)* No compassion. For the first time in three years, I desired a woman. He hated it!

DOCTOR   Three years? Why so long?

RANDOULF   That's the way he wanted it. Just me and him.

Randoulf 2 appears, calling. Randoulf tries to ignore it.

RANDOULF 2   Randoulf! Randoulf!

DOCTOR   What did you do for sex?

RANDOULF 2   Randoulf! *(Randoulf looks toward him)*

DOCTOR   Randoulf. *(He looks back at her)* Is anything wrong?

RANDOULF   Yes. I mean… as for sex…

DOCTOR   Yes.

RANDOULF   He said no woman is worthy of us.

RANDOULF 2   Let's masturbate?

RANDOULF   It was you.

RANDOULF 2   Who yuh expeck? Josephine?

DOCTOR   He's here?

RANDOULF 2   Yes.

RANDOULF   I was wondering how long it was going to take you to come back.

RANDOULF 2   Everybaddy mek harsh decisions some-times an mi noh different fram yuh. *(He flips and rolls into an upright position).* Aafta aal yuh created mi.

RANDOULF   Piss off!

RANDOULF 2   Dis is a fine welcome.

RANDOULF   I said piss off!

RANDOULF 2   A si seh shi hav arn lipstick. Dem a wok pan yuh mentality. A am back toh correct yuh.

RANDOULF   Take a good look at my surroundings... what do you see and what the fuck can you correct?

RANDOULF 2   A hav adder consciences who hav seen worse ...dem man an woman would seh yuh lucky.

RANDOULF   Lucky?

RANDOULF 2   Yes. I've seen somma di braddas an sistas dat a holiday would da doh dem juss fine but dem full dem wid drugs cause it cheaper dan lang periods aaf psychotherapy.

RANDOULF   Dr Kumar does not want to use drugs on me... she wants me in my natural state.

RANDOULF 2   Soh shi cyaan recommend dat yuh need dem.

RANDOULF   Rani wouldn't do something like that.

RANDOULF 2   Rani ah?

RANDOULF   Yes.

RANDOULF 2   A suppose yuh truss her?

RANDOULF   Yes.

RANDOULF 2   Like Josephine? *(Randoulf goes for him)* A juss waan fi show yuh, yuh still open fi hijacking.

RANDOULF   Tell him you mean me no harm. *(He moves closer)* Tell him.

DOCTOR   Where is he? *(He points to her right)*

RANDOULF   There! *(He moves behind her)* There! *(He gets under the bed)* Here, here, here!

DOCTOR   I... I mean him no ... Jesus Christ... *(under her breath)*...harm.

RANDOULF   See.

RANDOULF 2   Ask her if yuh woz being giing di wrang drugs deliberately, would shi document it an feed it toh yuh relatives?

RANDOULF   If I was deliberately given the wrong drugs would you document it and give it to my relatives?

DOCTOR   That... I cannot discuss with you.

RANDOULF 2   Tell her. I waan fi know wedda shi a treat one incident ar a multitude a people dat shi section pan her travels.

RANDOULF   She wants an honest assessment.

(Pause)

RANDOULF 2   A been toh sii Mummy. Shi still hav arn di same clothes shi did hav arn wen dem tek her weh. *(Randoulf bangs his head against the wall)* It painful mi know. Yuh waan si her now, shi looking into space continually.

RANDOULF   I don't..

RANDOULF 2   Shi nevah even recognise mi. Shi nevah coming out Randoulf.

RANDOULF   Rani?

DOCTOR   Yes.

RANDOULF   I haven't finished my adventure.

DOCTOR   Go ahead.

RANDOULF   I just need to finish the adventure. *(The Doctor puts on the tape recorder. A pause)* Josephine... came back... and all the emotions I fear came rushing over me... I told her I loved her and begged her to stop having sex with him ... I was so fucking stupid...

RANDOULF 2   Weh sweet nanny goat a goh run im belly.

RANDOULF   Yes I laid my cards on the table in one session and it felt good!

RANDOULF 2   Den wha happen? Shi ask yuh fi kill im.

RANDOULF   That was a cry for help.

RANDOULF 2   Aafta shi gi yuh di ting. Aafta shi quench yuh thirst, den an only den did shi cry fi help.

RANDOULF   Yes!

RANDOULF 2   Yuh remember weh yuh seh?

RANDOULF   Yes, yes, yes, yes, yes!

RANDOULF 2   Yuh noh langer living a life a self denial. Yuh deh pan yuh way toh recovery. Is my job fi get yuh out.

RANDOULF   Now I'm suppose to do a song and dance. *(claps his hands)*

RANDOULF 2   Yes an A will bang di tambourine an if wi cyaan manage it, wi will get her toh stamp her foot.

RANDOULF   I'd like this room given a full scale exorcism.

DOCTOR   Randoulf, I can't do that.

RANDOULF   I want him exorcised and this place, now! *(He grabs Randoulf 2 by the neck and slams him onto the bed)* I need a priest!

RANDOULF 2   Dis is nat looking good at aal.

RANDOULF   I couldn't give a fuck what it looks like!

RANDOULF 2   Relax!…

RANDOULF   Why did you leave?

RANDOULF 2   A woz coming out second bess aal di time. *(He releases his grip)* A hav been protecting yuh fi a very very lang time. Mi an yuh woz like dat. Remember Denise? Aal shi waanted woz fi dress yuh like yuh a dally. Right or wrang? Shantel, aal shi waanted woz a baby wedda it woz going toh bi yours only di devil would know. Now dat woz a hard one fi get rid av. A had toh gi yuh food poison, yes food poison, twice in one month, a nearly kill wi. Sonia, Angela, Sandra an Jill dem nevah hav di guts, dem did easy fi get rid aaf. Now Nicole shi woz di one dat A thought woz going toh bi di one.

RANDOULF   Why?

RANDOULF 2   Shi woz genuine. Shi actually did care bout yuh.

RANDOULF   Now you admit it, when the horse has bolted. You stay for Nicole and run for Josephine.

RANDOULF 2   Shi was a gutsy character. Shi had aal di proper tools. Intelligence, looks, charm an wit. *(Randoulf climbs into bed)* In fack shi woz betta dan mi in aal departments... dats wen aal di trouble started. Shi... Yes, shi would tempt yuh until yuh buckle. Randoulf... Randoulf. Yuh narh tark toh mi noh, time will tell. A here toh help yuh. *(climbs into bed with him)*

DOCTOR   Randoulf... *(She picks up tape recorder)* Patient has fallen asleep... time fifteen thirty... *(She walks to the bed)* It seems like we are coming to the end... our last session. At times it has been frightening and exciting. I believe he's more vulnerable, than dangerous. *(She stops the tape)* A woman who is willing and able to sustain a good fight physically, intellectually, and spiritually could wear him down. Yes. A woman like that would be ideal for him.

She looks in the mirror and her reflection begins to speak to her.

REFLECTION   Rani?

DOCTOR   Yes.

REFLECTION   We have come a long way, haven't we?

DOCTOR   We certainly have considering many moons ago all we used to eat and drink was goats' feet and sweet toddy. Yeuk. Now we eat steak, asparagus, salad and drink Chardonnay...

REFLECTION   But I still miss my rice boiled in a clay pot.

DOCTOR   I don't care… we need to bury it like an artefact. *(She applies lipstick)* Don't let it surface again…

REFLECTION   Getting ready for William?

DOCTOR   Yes. He was a lucky catch. Educated at Cambridge...

REFLECTION   …and has always wanted something dark and lovely. *(She pushes back her hair)* You love him?

DOCTOR *(steps back from mirror)* Of course I do. He's refined and privileged...

REFLECTION   We should be with our own.

DOCTOR *(touches the face in the mirror)* Listen peasant girl… when somebody finds you exotic – feed his ego…

REFLECTION   Well, I don't feel exotic. I feel like a servant girl.

DOCTOR   Well, I don't! *(She turns and looks at her figure)* He loves us, well me. Our bottom is too big.

REFLECTION   Our man likes something he can hold, not something that pricks him like nettles.

DOCTOR   Be gone...

Randoulf wakes.

RANDOULF   I was dreaming.

DOCTOR   About what? *(She turns tape on)*

RANDOULF   That he came back. *(turns the radio on)*

JULIAN *(shouting)*   Turn vat fucking music down you faggot!

The sound of banging from off-stage.

RANDOULF   The lunatic is there. The devil has arisen! *(He moves to the spy hole, opens the door)*

JULIAN   Listen mate... I'm a lover of music miself... What I'm trying to say is, can ya turn it down a bit?

RANDOULF   I'm sorry. I wasn't aware, it was that loud. I'll adjust the volume.

JULIAN   Fanks mate, I really appreciate it.

Randoulf closes the door and prepares the furniture for the arrival of Josephine and Julian. He then turns the music down and listens through the floor with a glass. Off-stage, we hear:

JULIAN   I went up there and put him in his place.

JOSEPHINE   Really?

JULIAN   What? Ya fink I'm lying?

JOSEPHINE   No, no. I'm glad you're my man. I feel so safe.

JULIAN   If Tony Blair can have a bodyguard why can't you?

RANDOULF   He needs a test of endurance. *(He turns the music up again)*

The bell rings loudly.

RANDOULF   Are you a police officer?

JULIAN   Look –

JOSEPHINE   Julian, don't...

RANDOULF   I'm going to close my door again so we can start all over... *(He closes the door and turns the music down. There is a soft knock. He opens the door)* ... hello.

JULIAN	I didn't mean to ring ya bell as hard as I did.
RANDOULF	We all make mistakes. How can I help you?
JULIAN	I was wondering…
RANDOULF	I'm Randoulf and *you* are?…
JULIAN	Julian...
RANDOULF	Look why don't you come in?… we are neighbours, after all. *(Julian and Josephine enter)*
JOSEPHINE	We were just about to eat.
JULIAN	See I told ya he was alright, didn't I Joe?
RANDOULF	Please, sit down. What would you like to drink?
JULIAN	Anyfing. I ain't fussy.
RANDOULF	And the lady?
JULIAN	She'll drink anyfing. Just give her what you give me.
RANDOULF	So, that's two brandies.
JULIAN	Ya don't mess about, do ya, mate?
JOSEPHINE	That'll be fine.
RANDOULF	Not if I can help it. It leads to people taking advantage. Sorry, that was to your man's question. *(handing drink to her, then one to Julian)*
JULIAN	Women... Give em an inch an' they walk all over ya. Cheers!
JOSEPHINE	Thank you.
RANDOULF	My pleasure.
JULIAN	Now don't embarrass me. Drink it slow…
JOSEPHINE	Julian... *(She shuts up)*
JULIAN	I ain't a hard man Randoulf. But I must wear the jeans, the pants and the overalls, ya know what

a mean? *(Randoulf nods)* I see you're a man like me. A ruler.

RANDOULF   I can see that. *(Josephine laughs nervously)* Josephine, is the drink alright? *(Josephine bows her head)*

JULIAN   Have you two met before?

JOSEPHINE   No.

JULIAN   How do ya know her name? *(Pause)*

RANDOULF   I can hear everything up here. *(tapping the floor with his foot)* That's why the music is up loud sometimes.

JULIAN   Everyfing?

RANDOULF   Yes. *(with a smile)* Everything.

JULIAN   Even…? *(Randoulf nods)*

RANDOULF   It's… embarrassing at times. *(They laugh)*

JULIAN   And I thought this place was sound proof.

RANDOULF   Would you like another brandy?

JULIAN   Yeah, why not? The night is young.

RANDOULF   Josephine? *(She looks up)*

JULIAN   She's a slow drinker. Women can't drink like men.

RANDOULF   True, but there is a scientific reason for that.

JULIAN   Oh yeah?

RANDOULF   Yes. Women have less water in their body than men.

JULIAN   You're a right brainy bloke, ain't ya Randoulf? I bet you read a lot?

RANDOULF   No, as a matter of fact, I listen to the radio. *(hands him drink)*

JULIAN   Radio? Cheers.

RANDOULF	Let's make a toast.
JULIAN	Yeah. Yeah. *(stands then sits again)*
RANDOULF	Please be my guest.
JULIAN	To... To... Josephine, what shall I toast to?
JOSEPHINE	How about... to good neighbours?
JULIAN	Yeah vat's a good one. To good neighbours!
ALL *(toasting)*	Cheers!

(Randoulf goes to top up Josephine's glass)

JULIAN   Joe.

JOSEPHINE   No thank you, one's enough for me.

JULIAN   Josephine is very sensible. She never over does anyfing.

RANDOULF   Everything in moderation, that's what I say. *(She crosses her legs)* So, what is your occupation? *(Julian coughs and Josephine uncrosses her legs)*

JULIAN   I borrow and lend.

RANDOULF   Yes.

JULIAN   Tell him.

JOSEPHINE   He borrows credit and lends it back at a profit?

RANDOULF   So, you're a businessman?

JULIAN   Yeah, somefing like vat. I wouldn't say no. *(Randoulf tops up his glass)* What game are you in?

RANDOULF   I design computer games.

JULIAN *(lights up)* Ya joking? *(Randoulf nods)* For Play Station and Nintendo? *(Randoulf nods)* Name me one of your games that you made.

RANDOULF   You wouldn't buy the kind of games I conjure up.

JULIAN   Your games don't get made do they? Your one a dem geeza's... What's vat computer nerd's name again?... *(He tries to get up)* Bill Clinton?… Bill Crate?…

RANDOULF   I know…

JULIAN   Bill Gates, the geeza who's got the computer market by the balls and pays people big dosh to lessen the competition by paying 'em uncreative money. *(A beat)*

JOSEPHINE   Julian…

RANDOULF   Alright. The last game I designed was *'Domestics.' (Julian's mouth drops. Josephine sits up)*

JULIAN   Ya joking?

RANDOULF   I'm not.

JULIAN   I got it downstairs, ain't I Joe? *(She nods)* All mi mates have vat game, you must be a millionaire, ya cunt.

RANDOULF   As long as you spread the word, I might become one.

JULIAN   Fuck me! *(He looks around, speechless)* Prove it ta me. *(Randoulf shows him the storyboard)* Fucking hell! He's the fucking creata. I can tell ya all about it. The bird's getting beat up and her little brother who's ten has to fight off everyone who has abused her and rescue his sister wivout injuring her or setting off the booby traps... I love the little fella... Zuri, he's cheeky and smart. *(He ponders)* He plays a keyboard and vat keyboard can turn into weapons and body armour when he plays the right tune.

JOSEPHINE   You must be...

JULIAN   Did I say ya could participate? Shud up! Did I say ya could speak?

JOSEPHINE   Sorry…

JULIAN   Ya betta be.

RANDOULF   I'm not accustomed to bullying.

JULIAN   She like's it when I let off like vat.

RANDOULF   Do you? *(No response)*

JULIAN   She ain't gonna say nuffin' unless I say so.

RANDOULF   I couldn't have a dumb woman around me. I like individual personality.

JULIAN   Well she ain't got none. Everyfing is mine.

RANDOULF   I can see that.

JULIAN   And vat's how our relationship works.

JOSEPHINE   I can speak for myself, thank you very much.

JULIAN *(laughs)* Did ya hear the little mouse? *(looking around)* Want a bit of cheese?

JOSEPHINE   I'm leaving you, you little prick. *(He laughs)* I mean it.

JULIAN   How many times have ya said vat?

JOSEPHINE   I mean it this time. Can I have another drink Randoulf?

JULIAN   I never said you could have another one.

RANDOULF   Are you sure this is a good idea?

JOSEPHINE   Yes. *(Randoulf fills her glass.)*

JULIAN   Take one sip and I'll break your face.

JOSEPHINE   Thank you. I'd like to make a toast.

JULIAN   To the blood that'll come from you.

JOSEPHINE   To the state of independence. *(She brings the glass to her lips)*

JULIAN   Don't mock me. I said don't mock me! *(She drinks. He slaps the drink away and is about to punch her, when Randoulf grabs him)*

RANDOULF   For Christsakes man, she's a woman.

JULIAN   Wiv a big mouth.
(Randoulf knees him in the groin and slams him to the floor)

RANDOULF   Look in the drawer, you'll see some rope. What are you waiting for?

JULIAN   Let me go. *(He struggles)*

RANDOULF   Calm down Julian…

JOSEPHINE   Which drawer? *(Randoulf punches him in the kidneys)*

RANDOULF   The top one. Hurry up. Quick, tie his hands.
(He holds his hands while she ties them up. He then gets him in a head lock lifting him off the floor and sits him on the chair while Josephine ties his feet to the chair)

JULIAN   When I get hold of you I'm gonna kill you! Panasonic! Panasonic! *(Barking off-stage)*

JOSEPHINE   Now – you bastard.

JULIAN   God help ya when I come outta vis.

JOSEPHINE   Who says your gonna get out?

JULIAN   What ya gonna do, kill me? *(He laughs)*

JOSEPHINE   I might... *(She listens)* … Your best friend cares about ya.

JULIAN   At least *he's* loyal.

JOSEPHINE   Are you alright darling?

RANDOULF   Absolutely.

JULIAN   Well lover boy, have I got news for you? She's not even a proper woman. She can't even have kids.

JOSEPHINE   I'm all woman. *(She slaps him)* You punched two babies out of me! That's right. Men like you don't care, so we can tell you anything and you believe us. *(She grabs him by the balls)*

RANDOULF   Don't you think you're going too far?

JOSEPHINE   I've only just begun. *(She punches him in the stomach)* You... you could never imagine the hate I had for you while you were on top of me... you should have seen him trying to excite me about doing it to himself... *(She gets the pillow from the bed)* The greatest thing a woman can give is her body... I gave you mine as a virgin, for you to care for... *(She stands behind him and covers his face with the pillow)* ...and all you did... *(He struggles violently)*...was club away at it... *(She holds his head and the pillow tightly to her chest)*

RANDOULF   Josephine, don't you think that's enough?

JOSEPHINE   Keep out of this, Randoulf. This is my fight. Isn't that so, woman beater? *(She removes the pillow)* One, two, three, four... *(She covers his face again)* Good. Good. Good. *(She removes the pillow)* You did this to me... *(She covers his face again for longer. He struggles)* ... Now you know what it feels like. *(She takes away the pillow, takes bottle of brandy and forces drink down his throat)* Now drink... You're spilling my friend's good brandy...

RANDOULF   He's choking.

JOSEPHINE   That's what he's supposed to do. *(He spits it out)* Don't spit out anymore or I'll ram it down deeper. *(She slaps him)*

RANDOULF   Jesus Christ Joe... his body won't be able to consume so much alcohol.

JOSEPHINE   This is what the bastard used to do to me... Drink, ya bastard... then he'd have sex with me while I was unconscious. *(She takes the bottle away)* I thought of other men while he was abusing me... *(She walks to Randoulf)* I'd think of this wonderful man. He'd beat me into submission, then... *(She gets knife and walks round him)*

RANDOULF   Women are supposed to be loved not punished. *(She stands beside Julian holding the knife at his throat)*

JOSEPHINE   May the devil meet you with open arms. *(Randoulf holds the knife with her)*

RANDOULF   Let me do it... my mother knew a man like him.

JULIAN   You'll... you... never get way wiv it.

JOSEPHINE   Together... I love you *(They kiss)*

Josephine pulls his head up and bares his throat. Randoulf cuts it slowly. Lights fade down slowly. They undress and get into bed.

JOSEPHINE   Let me tie your hands to the bed. *(No response)* Please... Please... *(She kisses him. He nods. She ties his hands and feet to the bed.)* I love you.

RANDOULF   I... love you too. I want to hold you.

JOSEPHINE   No. *(She kisses him)* I want to kiss you forever and ever.

RANDOULF *(panics)* Josephine...

JOSEPHINE   Yes.

RANDOULF   It's come off.

JOSEPHINE *(kissing him)* I know.

RANDOULF   Put it back on.

JOSEPHINE   No.

RANDOULF   Then get off.

JOSEPHINE   I'm free. We're free.

RANDOULF *(struggling)* Why?

JOSEPHINE   You love me. I love you and I want all of you.

RANDOULF   Get off! For godsakes Josephine – don't!

Blackout. Slowly lights fade up. Josephine is walking around. Randoulf is sitting on the bed.

RANDOULF   Why?

JOSEPHINE   You don't realise what you've done, do you?

RANDOULF   Why?

JOSEPHINE   You've killed for me. That's true love.

RANDOULF   Why?

JOSEPHINE   Look at him. I'm the last woman he put his hands on. *(He nods)* I won't be long. *(She kisses him)* Remember, I love you.

She exits. Lights fade up.

DOCTOR   Randoulf... Randoulf… *(She shakes him gently)* Randoulf…

RANDOULF   Yes.

DOCTOR   I understand your journey.

RANDOULF   Boy am I thirsty. Sorry… would you like a glass of water?... Hold on... *(He opens a cupboard)* … I have a bottle of water. *(He hands it to her)* Please accept my offer.

DOCTOR   Thank you.

RANDOULF   She never came back…
(Randoulf 2 appears but he refuses to acknowledge him.) I waited and waited. Paced up and down. Sang to myself hoping she'd return that minute, there and then. I turned my back on the body. He called my name, laughing at me, challenging me to look at him. I took the mattress from the bed and dumped it on him – still he laughed. Now he looked like a giant – growing and expanding with every second, pushing me away…

JULIAN   She can't even have kids. *(He laughs)*
She's not even a proper woman. I wear the jeans, the
overalls and the pants.

RANDOULF   Again and again I told him to shut up.
He said because he knew no better – it made him
innocent.

JULIAN   I'm in hell and the devil's here... there's
a place here for you and I can tell you, it's thirsty
work...

RANDOULF *(unties the body)* He's not really dead,
Mummy. Look I'll show you... I'll get some water and
clean him up... *(He gets water)* Within no time, he'll be
eating and walking about like normal... Soup – that's
what I'll give him, just like you used to give me when I
was ill... *(He tries to mop up the blood)* It looks worse
than it really is. Mummy, this is Julian. *(He sits him up
at the table)* Julian this is my mother. Don't show me
up, you little bastard. *(He lays him down)* Maybe he's
more sick than I thought... He's still bleeding... Mummy
it won't stop. Stop it!
(He puts his hand over the wound) Stop bleeding! *(He
gets a needle and stitches it up)* If I don't stitch you up,
you'll bleed to death. It's small. Yes... before long I'll
have you as good as new.
(He leans back, admiring his work)

Lights fade down slowly.

SCENE 3
*Randoulf has put Julian to sit upright at the table. He sits
opposite. Randoulf is eating while Julian's food remains
untouched. Julian is tilted to one side. The Doctor is
standing in the middle.*

RANDOULF   Stop posing and eat your meal… you're not with your buddies now. There are many hungry people in this world who'd appreciate that meal right now. I know we've been through this before… Anyway, tell me what you're going to say to the authorities. *(He listens)* You've got it wrong already. I'll brief you again! First of all, it was an accident. We were playing and you slipped… fell on the knife which I was holding… Right? Good, now eat up your food, it's getting cold. *(The sound of barking and footsteps. The bell rings.)* Tell them we're not at home. *(He pokes him)* Tell them. *(The bell rings)* Well, I'll do it. No one's home.

POLICE 1 *(off-stage)* Are you Mr Randoulf Temple?

RANDOULF   Yes, but he's not at home.

POLICE 1 *(off-stage)* Could you please open the door Mr Temple? We are police officers and we need to gain access to these premises.

RANDOULF   Can't you come back tomorrow?

POLICE 2 *(off-stage)* Mr Temple if you don't open the door we will have to break it down.

RANDOULF   You guys are so destructive. Alright, I'll open the door.

POLICE 1 *(off-stage)* We have a warrant to gain entry.

RANDOULF *(to Julian)* Fix yourself up, you make the place look messy. *(He opens the door. The police enter)*

POLICE 2   Jesus fucking Christ! *(He covers his mouth and nose)* What a stink.

RANDOULF   That must be the rubbish bin.

POLICE 1   Let's take him in…

They exit. Lights fade up slowly.

DOCTOR   We can treat you. You'll be able to see the outside world again. It's not something I would normally say to a patient.

RANDOULF   I used to hate her.

DOCTOR   Understandable.

RANDOULF   Now I think, if I was a woman I'd have done the same thing.

Randoulf 2 appears.

RANDOULF 2   Yuh learn di lesson di hard way an yuh still hav a heart.

DOCTOR   Would you agree to medication?

RANDOULF   As long as it wasn't postponing the inevitable.

DOCTOR   It's curable.

RANDOULF 2   A will care fi yuh, noh badda wid shi. Yuh noh need drugs, yuh juss need toh bi yuhself.

RANDOULF *(hiding)* When I needed you, you scarpered.

RANDOULF 2   Yuh noh gi mi weh fi one a dem.

DOCTOR   He's back? *(looks around)*

RANDOULF 2   Yes, wid unfinished business fi doh. Weh yuh a hide fa? A lizard yuh a eat?

DOCTOR   Pay no attention to him. Come out and sit down.

RANDOULF   I need some peace. I can't take anymore. The devil wants me.

RANDOULF 2   Yuh laas some a yuh screws since yuh?…

RANDOULF   No.

DOCTOR   You have to confront him.

RANDOULF 2   It look soh toh mi.

RANDOULF   He's too strong.

DOCTOR   You allow him to overpower you.

RANDOULF 2   A noh mi who waan feed im drugs, A waan fi gi im back toh im people.

DOCTOR   Take my hand. *(She gives him her hand)* Hold it. *(He does)* Now come. He'll get weaker. Good. *(She kneels down and encourages him to hug her)*

RANDOULF 2   I know aal di carners, yuh ears hard ee?

RANDOULF *(holding on very tight)* The burden has been great.

DOCTOR   Let it fall Randoulf... let it fall.

RANDOULF 2   Shi will hav yuh worshipping those purple, yellow an green pills, if yuh nat careful.

DOCTOR   Relax Randoulf... everything will be fine.

RANDOULF 2   Shi will lack yuh up fi good an prappa. *(He kneels beside her)*

DOCTOR   Alright? *(He nods)*

RANDOULF 2   Een here dem will....

RANDOULF   Piss off!

RANDOULF 2   No. Aal a oonoo who barn ya, oonoo ungrateful fi di blood weh spill fi oonoo.

RANDOULF *(covers his ears)* La... la... la... la... la...

DOCTOR   Sing the words Randoulf, sing the words.

RANDOULF 2   A will mek im sing loud an clear.

RANDOULF   I can't hear you.

RANDOULF 2   Yuh will. Fram di tree dem use fi hang wi fram, di noose tightly glued aroun wi neck, eyes dem a pop an tongue a swell as large as watta melons. While on-lookers dance an chatta wid delight.

RANDOULF   That has nothing to do with me. *(He puts the Doctor between himself and Randoulf 2)*

RANDOULF 2   But it could happen again.

DOCTOR   Ignore him.

RANDOULF 2   A could da come een darkness, an high jack yuh baddy while yuh sleep.

RANDOULF   I'm not afraid of the dark any more... *(He faces him)*... and further more I'm on the mend.

RANDOULF 2   Look pan mi.

RANDOULF *(goes to the door)* Out! Out! Out!

DOCTOR   Don't get worked up. Relax.

RANDOULF 2   Weh yuh si?

RANDOULF   I said get out!

RANDOULF 2   Freedom iz wha yuh should si.

RANDOULF   You imprisoned me... She gave me the opportunity to feel again! I am my own man. I am free!

RANDOULF 2   Yuh hav more freedom, dead!

RANDOULF   Well I've asked the dead and I...

RANDOULF 2   Did yuh ask Gad? *(Randoulf remembers)* Well? *(He picks up an old letter)* Di mail has arrive.

RANDOULF   Give it to me.

RANDOULF 2   Well, well, well. Wat a surprise, is fram her. Wha happen, someting sting yuh?

RANDOULF   You're lying. *(He turns to the Doctor)* The medication – is it ready and available?

RANDOULF 2 *(reading the letter but we hear Josephine's voice)* Interesting.

RANDOULF   Give it to me! *(He tries to grab it)* I said give it to me!

RANDOULF 2   Mek a read it fi yuh.

RANDOULF   I need those pills.

RANDOULF 2   Greetings from a tormented woman. Noh address. *(Randoulf sits on the floor and rocks)* It's been a long time but memories don't leave, like people do...

JOSEPHINE *(continuing)* Good treatment, that's all I wanted. I make no apologies for the need to survive.

You may not agree with my methods but self-help was
the only solution. I know you're on the receiving end...
and it's not justice but I can't elaborate further for
obvious reasons... I really did love you and still do.
Lots of love – J.

RANDOULF 2   P.S. God will help you Randoulf. After
all it is a/

JOSEPHINE   / man's world.

RANDOULF 2   Kiss, kiss, kiss... Dat's how many
kisses shi sen yuh. P.P.S. Our daughter... *(Randoulf
freezes)* ... is three years old tomorrow.

RANDOULF   Give it to me.

RANDOULF 2   Yuh tink a lie mi a tell?

RANDOULF   Gimme it! The stupid woman. She took
a daughter from me. I have a daughter. I have a
daughter? No! *(He tears up the letter)*

JOSEPHINE   Our daughter...

RANDOULF   No!

JOSEPHINE   Our daughter...

RANDOULF   I have a daughter for men to abuse!

JOSEPHINE   ...is six months old tomorrow.

RANDOULF   For men to undermine and put down!

RANDOULF 2   Shi a one a dem dat tek widout consent.

RANDOULF   God send her to hell for committing
such a wicked act!

RANDOULF 2   Yes.

RANDOULF   I have a daughter! I won't be there to
protect and guide her. *(throws his bedding on the floor)*

RANDOULF 2   Dem will hav her wearing weaves until
it look like bird ness. Straightening her hair, dyeing it
blonde, purple, pink an blue. If shi come out dark
enough dem will hav her bleaching her skin an wearing
lipstick red as cherries.

RANDOULF *(washing himself)* I'm clean! I had nothing to do with it!

RANDOULF 2   Dem will turn her against yuh. Dem will gi her work among dem. Praise pan how well shi fitting een an complimenting her fi one ting… Travelling home pan di tube shi wi feel proud, until shi enter fi her territory. Di passengers, skin colour change... now shi know who shi really is. Now shi begin fi despise her own features.

RANDOULF   None of this has happened!

RANDOULF 2   But it will.

RANDOULF   Can we stop it?

RANDOULF 2   If yuh ready fi di journey. Yuh ready?

RANDOULF   Yes.

RANDOULF 2   Gad is di key, soh yuh muss listen toh mi.

RANDOULF   What if I don't agree?

RANDOULF 2   A will repeat miself. Wi shall mek her intoh a Queen Hatshepsut.

RANDOULF   But they'll kill her.

RANDOULF 2   Shi will die wid pride an shi will bi remembered.

RANDOULF   I'm tired, so tired… I was in hell and he walked with me… Under her influence… I was a baby and she fed me… Under his influence he would have killed her… Under her influence, she made love to me. I shouldn't be here! Under their influence, we are forever fighting…

He lays down on the floor. Randoulf 2 kneels beside him.

RANDOULF 2   Now sleep.

The Doctor and guards enter.

RANDOULF 2   Relax… Don't move fi a year an wi will
      bi free.

The Guards pick up Randoulf and carry him out.

Randoulf 2 remains. He turns his head and looks at the audience.

Lights fade down slowly to black.

The end.

GLOSSARY

Jamaican	English
A	I
Aaf	Off
Ar	Or
Aredi	Already
Arn	On
Baggie	Knickers
Barn	Born
Bill	Build
Blin	Blind
Bout	About
Brok bad	Raised badly
Caal	Call
Carr	Cause
Craas	Cross
Cyaan	Can
Deh	There
Di	The
Dis	This
Doh	Do
Dong	Down
Drap	Drop
Dweet	Do it
Eeda	Either
Een	In
Enna	In your
Fardda	Father
Fart	Rubbish
Fi	For
Figetting	Forgetting
Foss	First
Gad/Gard	God
Gess	Guess
Gi	Give
Giing	Giving

Jamaican	English
Goh	Go
Gwan	Go on
Ha	Hay
Hol	Hold
Laas	Last
Lakka	Like
Lick	Hit
Luk	Look
Madda	Mother
Marrid	Married
Mek	Make
Mi	Me
Mine	Mind
Muss	Must
Nat	Not
Nevah	Never
Noting	Nothing
Out-ta	Out of
Pan	On
Pickney	Children
Raas	Bloody (hell)
Rahtid	Surprise
Saarf	Soft
Seh	Say
Shi	She
Sidong	Sit down
Sii	See
Somma	Some of
Somebaddy	Somebody
Stap	Stop
Strangga	Stronger
Suck-ka	Sucker
Taal	Tall
Tan	Stand
Taught	Thought

Jamaican	English
Tark	Talk
Tek	Take
Tinking	Thinking
Tohdeh	Today
Tong	Turn
Trangga	Stronger
Trew	Through
Trow	Throw
Undda	Under
Waan	Want
Wah	Way
Weh	Where
Wen	When
Wha	What
Wi	We
Wok	Work
Ya	Here
Yarh	Your
Yuh	You

Thank you to: *Imperial War Museum, Royal Opera House, South East London Community Foundation, Oval House, Womens Aid, Benji Reid, Karlos Coleman, Suzann Mclean, Tony, Paul Everitt, Marlon Richards, Marcia Hewitt, Ian Harry, Kate Hart, Deni Francis, Tom Cotterill, Samantha Nurse, Tony Battick, Young Vic Theatre.*

DID YOU KNOW?

- Black men are up to 10 times more likely to be diagnosed on first admission to hospital with schizophrenia than their white counterparts.
- One woman in nine is severely beaten by her male partner every year.
- Black men are more likely to be given higher doses of medication, and less likely to be offered counselling, than their white counterparts.
- 48% of female murders in Britain are the result of women being killed by their partners.
- Studies on mental illness in Jamaica, Barbados and Trinidad show rates of mental illness are the same for black people as for white British people, however rates of black mental illness are much higher in diasporic communities.
- 25% of all crime recorded is domestic violence.
- Britain has 200 times more sanctuary spaces for abandoned animals, than for women fleeing violent partners.

LONDON ARTS

Funded by
THE ARTS COUNCIL OF ENGLAND

Oval House

Is Living
in Britain
Driving
Black Men
MAD?

"UNDER THEIR INFLUENCE"
BY WAYNE BUCHANAN

A New Psychological thriller from
KUSHITE THEATRE COMPANY

10th May–3rd June
Tickets £5/£8 BOX OFFICE 020 7582 7680
OVAL HOUSE THEATRE, KENNINGTON OVAL SE11

Mind works for a better life for everyone with experience of mental distress.

The *Diverse Minds* programme was set up by Mind with support from the Department of Health, to make mental health services more responsive to the needs of people from black and minority ethnic communities.

Mind's policy on black and minority ethnic mental health calls for action - including improved information services, translation and interpreting services, training for mental health staff, reduced coercion into the psychiatric and criminal justice systems and support for black and minority ethnic organisations through campaigning, providing information and training.

Diverse Minds works in Mind in England and Wales to promote better mental health practice for black and minority ethnic communities.

We provide:
• a quarterly magazine highlighting issues around minorities and mental health
• Subsidies towards training or conferences
• Information about training and conferences
• Opportunities to become involved with black and minority ethnic network in mental health.

We would welcome your donation, however large or small.

Diverse Minds, responding to the needs of a diverse community

If you would like to become a member or for more information contact:-
Kiran Juttla
Diverse Minds Development Manager
Tel: 020 8215 2222

Mind 15-19 Broadway, London, E15 4BQ
Tel 020 8215 2218 Fax: 020 8522 1725
Registered Charity Number 219830

Mind
The Mental Health Charity